RAW COMBAT

THE UNDERGROUND WORLD OF
MIXED MARTIAL ARTS

RAW COMBAT
THE UNDERGROUND WORLD OF MIXED MARTIAL ARTS

JIM GENIA

CITADEL PRESS
Kensington Publishing Corp.
www.kensingtonbooks.com

CITADEL PRESS BOOKS are published by

Kensington Publishing Corp.
119 West 40th Street
New York, NY 10018

All Kensington titles, imprints, and distributed lines are available at
special quantity discounts for bulk purchases for sales promotions,
premiums, fund-raising, educational, or institutional use. Special book
excerpts or customized printings can also be created to fit specific
needs. For details, write or phone the office of the Kensington special
sales manager: Kensington Publishing Corp., 119 West 40th Street,
New York, NY 10018, attn: Special Sales Department; phone 1-800-221-
2647.

CITADEL PRESS and the Citadel logo are Reg. U.S. Pat. & TM Off.

First printing: November 2011

10   9   8   7   6   5   4   3   2   1

Printed in the United States of America

CIP data is available.

ISBN 13: 978-0-8065-3504-3
ISBN 10: 0-8065-3504-0

This book is dedicated to Gaby and Emmy,
my perfect wife and my perfect daughter.

Contents

Acknowledgments   ix

Tradition   1
New York   15
Peter   35
A Tale of Two Fight Shows   54
TSK   73
Tap Out   90
Lyman   110
James   131
Kimbo   152
Submission Attempts   176
BAMA Fight Night   192
Epilogue   203

Acknowledgments

Thanks to Farley and Richard, an agent and an editor who believed. Thanks to Dale Peck, Peter Carey, and Roger MacBride Allen, three writing instructors who bade me to not suck. And a very special thanks to everyone who's ever stepped into the ring or cage and fought, bled, won, and lost. The word *inspiration* doesn't quite describe it, but it comes close.

RAW COMBAT

THE UNDERGROUND WORLD OF MIXED MARTIAL ARTS

TRADITION

I paid thirty bucks to the big, burly man at the door and walked into the South Bronx boxing gym unsure what to expect. It was February of 2003 and I was playing the role of curious spectator, my hidden notepad and pen and digital camera the only indicators otherwise. Around me sat a few dozen in bleachers, some of them cheering, all of us transfixed by the ring in the center of the room and the occupants within. And when the judo black belt in traditional kimono had his arm suddenly and violently twisted and broken by the kickboxer clad only in Lycra shorts, that was it. The New York underground fight scene had me hooked. It was beautiful, a poetry of violence, calligraphy with karate for brushstrokes and jiu-jitsu for ink.

Seven years and close to thirty editions of something called the Underground Combat League, watching hundreds of men throw everything they had at each other, and from the start I knew was gazing upon something special. If you live in the Five Boroughs, the UCL is the only game in town, the only place to see a Five Animal-style kung fu instructor get clobbered by someone who knows how to fight for real, the only place to see a personal trainer from the David Barton Gym on his hands and knees, blood leaking from his forehead and mouth and dotting the canvas. The UCL, not the first but for sure the most resilient, what you'd get if you made *Fight Club* a sport (but don't ever call it "Fight Club"; doing that shows how much you don't really know) and gave the thing a life of its own, made it a magnet for thugs looking to pound someone, for aspiring fighters and wannabes, for the ignorant and disillusioned, for the psychotic. A tradition, like when they'd gather in dojos in post-feudal Japan and scrap, or when they'd meet in back alleys in Brazil or under tents at fairgrounds in Europe, only a modern, up-to-date version where the party crashers wear blue uniforms and carry Glocks. A tradition, practically a Big Apple institution, and when mixed martial arts is legalized there will be no more need for it.

Puchy the bouncer (*left*) taking on a Five Animal kung fu instructor. (*Jim Genia*)

On a Sunday night I'm there, at the edge of a boxing ring somewhere in the Outer Boroughs. An endless array of cheap multicolored event posters cover the walls, warped and pitted floorboards squeak with each footfall, and the faded blue Everlast canvas stinks like meat gone spoiled, a side of beef long on dried blood and tetanus. Close by is a diminutive 135-pound Brazilian Jiu-Jitsu black belt named Emerson, there in the ring, so close I could reach out and touch him. He's an instructor, and his students present number over a hundred, a hundred and they've vacated the bleachers to crowd around the ring, a mad rush in the seconds before combat. If anyone is cheering for the karate fighter from Harlem, it's lost, whispers amidst crashing ocean waves. The referee yells "Go!" In the span of thirty-six seconds the Brazilian takes his opponent down, straddles him, and rains down punches until the karateka taps the canvas with his hand indicating *"No mas, no mas!"* It's all over but for the mayhem of celebration, and the tableau is so stunning, so charged and evocative, it could be a Caravaggio hanging in the Louvre.

Vale tudo, they had called it in Brazil in the 1900s (Portuguese for "anything goes"), but by the end of the century it was called something else here in the States, sometimes Ultimate Fighting or, disparagingly, human cockfighting, and now mixed martial arts (MMA) since the outrage over the spectacle has faded. The entire world went nuts over a SpikeTV reality show involving aspiring fighters battling it out in a cage called the Octagon, a more palatable thrill easier to swallow, and it's legal to hold such matches in Nevada, California, New Jersey—legal almost everywhere but New York. And I'm here thanks to a clandestine text message revealing time and place, clandestine because the New York State Athletic Commission isn't too keen on these sorts of shindigs.

The karateka and the Brazilian shake hands and hug,

according each other all sorts of respect and gratitude. The vanquished is as much a victim of the Brazilian's technique as of his own outdated training methodologies (punching and kicking imaginary opponents usually gets you a big fistful of fail), and he'll never step into the ring unprepared again. But it isn't about who wins or who loses as much as it's about the intensity of the battle, and this one has provided all with an up-close and hugely satisfying dose of it. In Las Vegas, superstars like Brock Lesnar and Randy Couture are captivating millions from within the cage of the Ultimate Fighting Championship, but here, at the lowest levels and in the trenches, the frontline skirmishes are all about local heroes giving it everything they've got and giving fans of fighting a glimpse of the reality of *mano a mano* combat.

Peter Storm is the man behind it all. Some say he's a villain, his secret events in ghetto-tastic boxing gyms deservedly criminal. But he's just someone you eventually stumble across if you live in the Big Apple and tote around a love for all things fighting. In the fourteen years since the first UFC graced the pay-per-view airwaves, promoter wannabes have sunk millions into organizations that crashed and burned and failed in spectacular fashion, but Peter took aim at a target more attainable, aimed square at the demographic hungry for intimate and personal action and an atmosphere of "Holy crap, these are some badass underground fights!" A feint, a body blow, and then a bare-knuckle hook to the chin and he's scored a knockout.

"We've never had a problem with the athletic commission or the police," he tells me, alluding to more of a "catch me if you can" than a "go ahead, try to shut me down, motherfucker" way of thinking. For Peter has never and would never advertise. You're either on his list to get a text message or you're not—and if not, the only way you'll ever know there was a UCL event last weekend is if your friend fought or maybe, just maybe, you scour the Internet for MMA-dedicated news sites and find results. It's the Keyser Soze of fight shows.

Peter (*right*) taking on a street fighter. (*Jim Genia*)

At mixed martial arts events in states where sanctioning is a way of life, where an athletic commission official oversees the urine samples for drug screening and someone with a conscience—or at least a concern about tort law—has matched up the competitors, the fighters will be more or less athletes of near-equal degrees of skill and commitment. But at an underground show anything goes and there are no weight classes. So if you agree to face someone with a hundred pounds on you, well, more power to you, brother.

Who are these people willing to risk their health and well-being in the unsanctioned wilds of unarmed combat? At a

New York City underground show, words like *motley crew, varied assortment,* and *wretched hive of scum and villainy* barely scratch the surface.

On one Sunday afternoon in June, at a martial arts school in Midtown, the cast of characters includes a massive Puerto Rican judoka, a lithe black boxer from Gleason's Gym, a short kickboxer from Jackson Heights, and a scrawny Tae Kwon Do practitioner. This UCL installment doesn't have the benefit of a boxing ring, so the forty-five or so spectators sit in white molded-plastic chairs around a large blue mat scarred with what could be a century of use. Peter, the maestro in the judo uniform, roams the room while his right-hand man, an amiable Hispanic named Jerry, talks of the task of rounding up competitors. If Peter is the bad cop in the equation, Jerry is the nice one who offers you coffee and hears your confession.

"The fighters who normally compete at these shows already know about mixed martial arts and most of the time they contact us because they want to fight," Jerry says. "Certain traditionalists are the ones that I find it hard to explain it to, because a lot of them have unrealistic thoughts of fighting," he says, alluding to every karate or kung fu practitioner rigid in their beliefs that all that's needed to win lies within one esoteric and outdated martial style.

"To be honest," Peter interjects, "we find a lot of guys who just want to fight." Or, more accurately, those guys find him.

Most aspiring combatants know how to find Peter. When not working nightclub security, he teaches private lessons at a school in Manhattan called the Fighthouse that rents out space to a wide variety of martial arts instructors, a repository of senseis without dojos of their own. It's a point of convergence for almost everyone who's ever donned a gi, slipped on padded gloves, and stuck a battered *Bruce Lee's Fighting*

Method into their knapsack. If you're interested in MMA in the Five Boroughs, one way or another, your path will lead you to him.

Today's match-ups would seem set to answer the age-old question of "Which style is best?" and Jerry informs me they're waiting on a fighter named Manny to arrive, Manny the ace in the hole, Manny the supposedly baddest man on the roster. In the meantime, the boxer from Gleason's Gym takes on the kickboxer from Jackson Heights, a fisticuff that deteriorates into something resembling a mugging, ending only when the boxer lands a right cross that drops his opponent, the boxer refraining from taking his foe's wallet and instead breathing a deep sigh of relief. The massive Puerto Rican, nervous and sweaty and a nightclub security worker himself, is up next, and he needs just a minute and a half to hyperextend his opponent's arm and force capitulation. Someone in the crowd shouts, "Break his fucking arm!" but that never comes to pass. (The Puerto Rican tells me his lady gave birth the night before and he got no sleep.)

There's a lull in the action and I'm informed that they're still waiting on Manny, Manny the heretofore unheard of Hercules and Gilgamesh of New York. Meanwhile, the scrawny Tae Kwon Do fighter squares off against someone called Iron Will, Iron Will shirtless and possibly even scrawnier than his opponent, like the "after" photo of someone who spent a few years on meth. The audience is subjected to frantic images of a cartoonesque melee, with all the chaos and flying limbs, and the Tae Kwon Do man goes down from a kick to the groin. There are only four rules of engagement in this league, practical restrictions labeled as "gentlemanly," and they are: no biting, no eye-gouging, no fish-hooking, and no groin strikes. The bout is ruled a "no contest," although things could've

Two street fighters squaring off at the second UCL. (*Jim Genia*)

played out much differently if these underground fighters had deigned to wear cups.

And then Manny finally arrives, and Iron Will introduces him to me as someone who could "kick everyone's ass out there." The clouds fail to part and sunshine does not blind us all. I size him up as a battered-looking kid who's eaten too many knuckles, and I ask him if he's going to fight.

"Nah," Manny says with a shake of his head. Manny is a pipsqueak who probably looks impressive hopped up on cocaine and swinging with reckless abandon, but at something shy of a buck-forty, with gangly limbs and a gaze about as sharp as cotton, he isn't much to look at now. "I'd kill these guys. But I've already been knocked out by bouncers twice this week, and I'm supposed to go to jail in a few days. I don't want to get there all messed up."

"Good thinking," I say, and if my expression or tone is outwardly sarcastic, I have no reason to believe he'd pick up on it. If the first rule about these events is to never talk about them, somewhere else on that list is to never believe someone's hype. It's only legitimate—only real—if you see it happen.

For another UCL event it's the same location but a slightly different cast. The turnout is low, dismal in fact, yet perfect for a small martial arts club from Battery Park City to mix it up with a wrestler, a pro fighter, and a ticking time bomb of a psychopath. Said psychopath wears a white karate uniform with a white belt and a yellow yin-yang patch on his chest, and his red-rimmed eyes are furtive and point to either an awful lot or an awful little going on in his head. Peter introduces him as Lamont Tareyton, but when he makes the papers, the *New York Daily News* will call him Tareyton Williams, a.k.a. "The Subway Saw Guy."

Lamont Tareyton Williams has no mixed martial arts training to speak of, but the story of him working as a barback at

Lamont Tareyton (*right*), ready and able—just not willing. (*Jim Genia*)

a South Bronx strip club and single-handedly destroying a group of rowdies when security couldn't get the job done warrants an invite from Peter. And here, now, Lamont's showing that he's got enough raw talent to dodge the Battery Park City fighter's best and deliver a near-knockout right hand—which he follows up with a stream of apologies.

"I'm sorry, my brother. I'm sorry." Lamont doesn't like that he's just hurt his opponent, or maybe the sudden violence has flicked a switch or come dangerously close to something inside that needs very badly to be left alone, and when he shakes his head and steps off the mat, kicking over a bag of foam sparring gear, he says he's done. No amount of encouragement from Peter, Jerry, or even from his opponent can convince him to change his mind. He's done. No more. He sits down in a gray metal folding chair, and I walk over and tell him that it's okay, that he looked good out there and that fighting isn't necessarily for everyone.

Lamont Tareyton (*left*) about to lose it. (*Jim Genia*)

"Thank you, my brother," is all he says.

Eleven days pass and Lamont wanders into the 110th Street subway station at 3:30 A.M. carrying a stuffed gorilla. According to police reports, Lamont, who's gulped down a bottle of Nyquil and has been suffering from blackouts, snatches a power saw from transit workers and does his best to carve up a stranger before fleeing into the night. He's caught hours later, and after passing a psychiatric examination that deems him fit for trial, he's eventually sentenced to eighteen years in prison. Present at the sentencing is Lamont's sixty-four-year-old victim (who miraculously survived). Lamont apologizes to him, right there in the courtroom, apologizes for what he's done and the pain he's caused, and the man—who suffered broken ribs and a punctured lung in the attack—accepts.

When Lamont is first apprehended, and his tale of insanity and violence is all over the news, Peter calls me on my cell phone, full of shock and disbelief that this nut job, this madman with a power saw, turned out to be Lamont, and that maybe, just maybe, we'd all been in some kind of danger that day he'd refused to continue fighting.

With Frankie the UFC champ (who had his first fight in the UCL and is the New York City underground circuit's most distinguished and accomplished alum) on one end of the spectrum and then Manny and Lamont on the other end, the range in the middle encompasses the vast majority of who you'll see fighting, the college students, blue collar workers, devout martial artists, and true believers. Their motivations run the gamut as well, some wanting to give "this whole fighting thing" a shot because they saw it on TV, some of them eager to test their skills, to see if their XYZ brand of karate really does hold all the secrets like they were told. They want to see if that assistant coaching position they have at Rutgers translates into badassery, or if the medal they got doing Greco-Roman at the Empire State Games means a damn. And some just like to hurt people, to get into a good fistfight, to feel a right cross against their face and hold an icepack to their swollen lip when everyone else is eating cheap slices of pizza at the place down Third Avenue later on that night.

It's all there in the New York City underground, a microcosm of brutality, a snapshot of what's going on in the rest of the world, a world exposed to the poetry and art and just plain beauty revealed in the cages and rings where sanctioned mixed martial arts bouts with rules are playing out. It's more than simply fighting. It's tradition.

Because whether there are rules or not, sanctioning or not, acceptance or not, they're still all taking part in something far greater, a ritual, handed down since men first gathered in a circle and cheered on the two in the center testing themselves. There's no room for hate there, no room for anything but respect, because it's coded into the sport regardless of whether the fight is *vale tudo* or sanctioned with a list of rules a mile long. Go ahead, watch them fight and try their damndest to hurt each other, and then watch them afterward. Invariably, those two fighters locked together in that dance of white-hot violence only moments before will shake hands or hug, a contrast to end all contrasts and a transaction of mutual respect when one would normally expect the market to be closed. Words unspoken, "Thank you for kicking my ass," "No, thank you for letting me," and there it is, the core of it all, the bushido that sagely Japanese masters spent lifetimes trying to impart upon their students. Nowhere else would you even think to express gratitude for a beat down and mean it, really mean it from the bottom of your heart, and nowhere else would it be cool and admirable and worthy of applause.

The degree of passion and emotion invoked when leather meets face and blood gets spilled verges on the ridiculous— you couldn't measure it if you tried—and yet there's the post-fight embrace, plain as day and impossible. It occurs, naturally like some genetic imprint, in the UFC before an audience of cheering (or booing) thousands, at a mid-level Ring of Combat event in a casino in Atlantic City before a packed crowd, and in a UCL before a scant fifty.

Only twice have I seen aberrations, once when Richie Torres outclassed a street fighter, when the referee pulled Richie off from on top of him the kid saw the ref holding Richie and wanted to keep going, maybe get some good licks in. The other time was Sekou Mau-Mau, a man with tattoos covering his face, who could've walked off the set of *300* as a member of Xerxes' elite guard. He, too, wanted more, didn't like that his karate-stylist opponent could dispatch him so easily, but then that's what referees are for, to jump in between (and yes, there are referees, even in underground fights).

Once, the emotion of battle overtook those watching, overtook two fight teams around a ring at a UCL in Queens, so vested in the outcome of the main event and entrenched in their status as brothers in arms to each of the main eventers were these students from rival schools that they began menacing each other, hurling insults and threats and promises. Too much for Peter, who climbed into the ring and halted the action, telling them firmly that if they didn't calm the fuck down the bout was off and everyone could go home. In that instance the fighters in the ring interjected, plucking out their mouthpieces and yelling to their teammates, "Look, see? It's okay. It's cool," and hugging each other right then and there. "It's just a fight." Just a fight, and that seemed to do the trick. Everyone took it down a notch. When time ran out and one fighter was awarded the decision, there was no rumble. There was only peace and respect.

Looking back, I realize that there could've been no other outcome. Tradition—fistic, brutal martial tradition—ultimately breeds harmony. Even at underground shows.

NEW YORK

In 1995 the traveling circus known as the UFC came to Buffalo, and all was well and good because few paid enough attention to this fringe fad to care that it was raw carnage and pure Fall of the Roman Empire madness. That changed by UFC 12 in 1997, however, changed like temperate political winds can change, and suddenly any professional incarnation of ultimate fighting (the generic label of "mixed martial arts" had yet to take hold) in New York was outlawed. The UFC fled to Alabama, packed everything up overnight when all signs pointed to the Empire State being a lost cause, and New Yorkers hungry for more of this thing that fascinated them on pay-per-view, this thing that piqued their interest in combat sports, were left screwed. There was, of course, New Jersey, where a trip across the Hudson River could yield an unsanctioned show run by Big Dan in a high school gymnasium somewhere, and maybe there was the occasional bout on one of Lou Neglia's Long Island kickboxing cards. But until New Jersey State Athletic Control Board Commissioner Larry Hazzard Sr. and his chief counsel Nick Lembo penned the Unified Rules, until the UFC's change in ownership (Dana White and Zuffa, LLC, are actually the franchise's second owners) and dramatic return from pay-per-view banishment, there wasn't much. New York was left a wasteland, a place where matches in a nightclub off the Long Island Expressway and shows at a Russian hotspot in Brooklyn were shut down, and the official stance of the athletic commission was "seek and destroy."

Peter's UCL came in 2003, the lone, steady offering, and because of its size (miniscule) and scope (pretty damn miniscule), it was untouchable by the authorities. Like an Al Queda terrorist cell of one. (For maintaining a mailing list of online acquaintances interested in attending UCL events, I was sent a cease-and-desist letter by the athletic commission instructing me to stop putting on these illegal shows; Peter got a laugh out of that one.) But by 2007, with the UFC and MMA more popular than ever, the ice began to melt. There were lobbyists at work, whispers of behind-the-scenes discussions and rumors of the possibility of a policy shift, and in 2008, New York State Athletic Commissioner Melvina Lathan, a firm but friendly woman and a fan of MMA, was named commission chairwoman. Now the powers that be in Albany are on the cusp of legalizing mixed martial arts, which will allow the Ultimate Fighting Championship into Madison Square Garden and throw open the floodgates holding promoters back from drowning the Empire State in fight shows. The world of unsanctioned matches—in timeworn rings in East New York, in basements in Inwood, on mats at kung fu schools in Midtown—is a world that's about to die.

Sands in an hourglass, running out, and you can blame progress for that, the same progress that saw a spectacle known as the Ultimate Fighting Championship banned from nearly every state and run off of television. The same progress that saw the UFC barely survive its dark years, you were lucky then if you could find a bar with a satellite TV subscription within driving distance, otherwise, watching any MMA was next to impossible. But the organization—the torch-bearer of the sport—kept alive the flame, and when Dana White and company took over, public opinion slowly but surely turned. Presently, just about everywhere under the sun wants MMA around (and the juicy direct and indirect revenue those events generate), and New York has entered into a seemingly perpetual state of legislative motion, the bills to legalize such fighting events inching interminably toward reality. And when that happens, when it's suddenly kosher to compete in mixed martial arts and there's the inevitable flood of promoters and their various Ultimate Extreme Totally Frickin' Awesome Championships, what then for the under-ground? There are no illicit shows in New Jersey, where the sport is fully sanctioned at both the pro and amateur level. An underground show there would be redundant, useless, tits on a bull. If Prohibition made kings out of bootleggers and the Volstead Act made them obsolete, so, too, will sanctioning affect New York's underground fight circuit.

But Peter, and a few others, still had time.

It was six months since the last UCL, a condition imposed upon New York City MMA fans due to either athletic com-mission pressure or Peter being forced to lay low after beating someone with a hammer (or a combination of both, accord-ing to our phone conversation). In the state's capital of Albany, the bill to legalize the sport had just jumped its biggest hurdle in the Assembly, where legislators in the com-mittee that had killed it the year prior had reversed their posi-tion and voted for a world of more fist-meets-face by a margin of fourteen to six. Things were so close you could taste it, so close you could hear the measured breaths and sense the tensed muscle of promotions both big and small, of the UFC and Ring of Combat, coiled and ready to leap onto the virtually untouched and fertile ground of the Empire State. But the concurrent bill in the State Senate, which had to make the rounds before the governor could affix his stamp of approval to make it law, had been stalled thanks to an unrelated political coup. Now it was a mystery as to when anyone would see sanctioned MMA in the state. Late 2009? 2010? Ask an assemblyman's director of legislative affairs or a state-appointed commissioner, an industry insider or veteran politico, and the answers would vary. Yet the one thing concrete was that right now the diminishing sands in the top half of the hourglass had been frozen. It was six months since the last UCL. Meanwhile, another event popped up in Brooklyn.

I made my way via subway to the worst, most crime-ridden neighborhood within the Five Boroughs, unsure of what to expect but ready for anything, ready for what could amount to nothing more than glorified sparring matches. The line stretching outside the boxing gym on this warm and sunny Saturday afternoon, however, implied that what awaited was something else entirely. If not for the Internet equivalent of word-of-mouth, I would have had no clue this event was going on, and I had to talk my way in, explaining that yes, I was a reporter, and this here magazine—and I handed them the current issue of *Full Contact Fighter*—was my employer. Heads were scratched, intentions were scrutinized, but ultimately I was allowed in to observe. Snap pictures. Take notes. Ask questions.

It wasn't *vale tudo* by any stretch, the fighters bedecked in shin pads and headgear and the action peppered with restarts galore whenever the requisite grappling inadvertently popped someone's headgear off. But it was something. "Martial Arts

Madness" was the official moniker, the madness mitigated by the organized staff (a staff!) employed for this family-run affair. At the helm was Sammy, a twenty-year-old karate exponent and self-proclaimed "USA-Peru Goodwill Ambassador," who flitted about anxiously in his suit and tie, assisted by his nineteen-year-old sister in a dress, his mother, who recoiled with disgust at every knockout, and his father, who smiled and shook hands and put out fires wherever they arose. They were friendly, and when there was a lull they handed me a plate of *arroz con pollo* with plantains—one part kind gesture, one part nod to this family from Queens ethnicity. At a table beside the ring two judges sat, in suits and ties as well. I asked them their backgrounds. One was a karate black belt, the other a kung fu black belt. Ring card girls in bikinis posed before a photographer's lens prior to the event's start, a full-fledged photo shoot while a few feet away fighters warmed up by shadowboxing and kicking and punching focus mitts.

About a hundred spectators filled the rows of metal folding chairs or stood lining the back, their presence crowding the venue and edging the success-o-meter's needle toward "win." Miraculously, the audience applauded when a small but in-shape kid climbed into the ring to open the event with a choreographed routine involving kitschy Asian bladed weapons and jumps and faux-purpose—really, an anachronistic tribute to end all anachronistic tributes and right up there with breaking boards. But when he exited and was replaced by fighters, the audience applauded even more.

Despite my intimacy with the city's underground fight scene, I didn't recognize any of the competitors, and their nicknames—"Blackie Chan," "The Tiger," "The Asian Submission Machine," and "The Flash Master"—hinted at fiercer lyrical battles than fights. Yet they fought hard in their own way, products of an Internet-and-SpikeTV generation's grab at glory with half-assed home training or ill-suited martial style backgrounds. The lanky Blackie Chan survived an early beating to eke out a decision. Tony the Tiger from Michigan brought the full fury of his Tae Kwon Do spinning-kick arsenal down upon a Goju Karate stylist to earn a second-round stoppage. A fighter grabbed one of Jarrett McBride's kicks and planted a punch square in McBride's chops, knocking him out. The diminutive Asian Submission Machine fell to a Shotokan Karate rep.

"Where did you find your fighters?" I asked Sammy during an intermission. The audience now milled about, noshing on chicken or sipping from bottles of water, while those who had fought mingled, their demeanors a mix of relief and pride.

"Tryouts," Sammy said, though later Jarrett McBride would tell me he's from Rochester and that Sammy had contacted him after seeing a fight of his on YouTube.

"Why the headgear?" I asked. Years before, I had spoken to UFC referee "Big" John McCarthy about the ins and outs of safety and how, when New York first went down the crapper, the idea of fighters wearing headgear had been bandied about. Big John was against that, reason being that headgear was something an opponent could grab and twist—and inadvertently snap a neck.

Sammy hemmed and hawed. In a few minutes someone was going to get in the ring and hand him a contrived award, like "Best Martial Artist Ever" or "All-Around Nice Guy," some form of self-congratulatory masturbation promoters at all levels are occasionally guilty of. "These are exhibition bouts," he said, as if that label alone somehow made it all okay.

A 250-pound Muay Thai practitioner named Dale squared off against a 240-pound wrestler nicknamed the "Savage." Dale had thick, meaty, tree-trunk legs, and as the Savage cautiously stepped forward, one of those legs came up and nailed him in the back of the head. Eight seconds from start to finish. The Savage was out cold, face-first on the canvas. Beside me, Sammy's mother cringed like she had just witnessed a murder.

One of the judges scampered into the ring, some sort of medical bag in hand. The Savage was slow to rise, but eventually he did, and left with all the grace of a newborn calf.

Next, the Flash Master outlasted a Tae Kwon Do rep after nearly three rounds of back-and-forth, the Tae Kwon Do rep exhausted, sitting with his arms limp at his sides and his head bowed. The judge with the medical bag returned to hold ice to the back of his neck. Then two 145-pound teenage teammates engaged, their coach cornering the one called Santiago and a hefty Latino in an orange shirt cornering the one called Romeo. Santiago flicked out his leg and it slapped Romeo's thigh, pulled it back to rechamber, flicked it out again but aimed higher. Romeo took Santiago's shin square in the face and he crumpled, fell limp through the ropes, somersaulted, and hit his forehead on the judges' table. He landed on the concrete floor like a body tossed from the back of a speeding van. There was a sharp and sudden collective gasp from the audience, the officials, the staff, and especially Sammy's mother. Six seconds was all this bout took, and the Latino in the orange shirt was too shocked to do anything other than stand there, horrified, his hands pressed to his head in a panic. The judge with the bag eventually got Romeo back to his feet, and when his headgear was removed the teenager managed a weak smile. The ring announcer thrust a microphone in his face and asked him how he felt, an absurd question for an absurd moment. "I feel good," Romeo said feebly.

The show was over, and like satisfied lovers the audience filtered out into the street, smoking, recalling moments exhilarating and shocking.

I was on the subway now, riding in the same car as Jarrett McBride and his friends and the hefty Latino in the orange shirt. The Latino was soft and friendly looking, as if he should have had a half-dozen children jumping and crawling all over him, calling him "Papi." Gone was the expression of horror. Now he couldn't stop laughing.

I held up my BlackBerry and showed him the photo I had snapped of Romeo tumbling out of the ring and him looking on in dismay. He laughed even harder. He was from Flushing and Romeo was a friend of his daughter's, and as Sammy had required that Romeo have a corner man, and Romeo's coach was in the corner of his opponent, the hefty Latino stepped in knowing nothing about the actual athletics of MMA, just knowing that he liked whatever UFC he'd seen on TV.

"I looked at my watch for a second. Then I look up and the kid is falling out of the ring." He shook his head. "I thought he was dead! I barely even know him and I thought I just seen him get killed." We laughed together at the sheer comedy of his situation. "I was just there as a favor," he said. "I don't know nothing about fighting!"

11

Assemblyman Bob Reilly became the face of the opposition in New York State with the simple act of standing up and spewing myths at a crucial time, when the bill to legalize MMA was in his Assembly committee—the Committee on

Tourism, Arts, and Sports Development—and a vote was taken before all ducks had been neatly gathered together in a row. It was 2008, and by this time New Jersey, Nevada, California, and nearly every other state with a viable athletic commission had hopped on the MMA train, and the Empire State was the last big holdout, the lone straggler, the crown jewel in the center of the media universe, a piece of fruit ripe and ready for picking. But Zuffa-driven lobbyist machine notwithstanding, all it took was for Assemblyman Reilly to ponder aloud, "We ban cockfighting and dog fighting—should we allow humans to enter a cage to knee, kick, and punch each other?" With those sentiments the bill was shelved and the people of New York were relegated to a few more years of unsanctioned underground shows. With those words, oldtimers around since the first UFC were reminded of a United States Senator named John McCain, who had waged a crusade against what he had dubbed "human cockfighting," a crusade that ended with the UFC banned in most states and exiled from cable television.

Senator McCain was everything fans of the emerging combat endeavor hated then: old, possibly under the influence of the boxing establishment, unable or unwilling to see the diamond in the rough, and the embodiment of "Whatever, dude, you just don't understand." And if you were to hop into a time machine to travel back and ask a 1997 MMA fan what hurt more, the fact that McCain was successful or the fact that, at that point in history, maybe McCain was at least partially right, well, the answer would contain venom, curse words, and an awful lot of anguish.

But it was a whole new world now, a whole new world thanks to the Unified Rules, the successes of Zuffa's version of the UFC, and the transformation of the spectacle of brawlers and sumo wrestlers getting kicked in the teeth into a legitimate sport. By 2008, you had to be seriously out of touch with pop culture to not be aware of what mixed martial arts had become.

In the ramp up to New York State's drive to legalize MMA, battle lines were drawn between Assemblyman Reilly and the lawmakers in favor of the bill that would repeal the ban, lawmakers armed with Zuffa-commissioned studies and courted and guided by the expert hands of former Nevada State Athletic Commission bigwig (and now UFC employee) Marc Ratner. At a legislative roundtable in Manhattan, Ratner shook my hand and assured me, "We'll get this thing done," and there was no question of "if" after he said that. It was all about the "when."

Still, Assemblyman Reilly fought on, dodging discourse and reason, seemingly very happy his phone was suddenly ringing with interview requests. "One way or another, he's sitting on the bill and making sure it doesn't go any further, and doing everything in his power to combat the sport," said Brian, a fighter who was featured on a season of reality show *The Ultimate Fighter*. It was December, and Brian had called me while on the road, excited yet cautious after having met with Assemblyman Reilly at the politician's Albany office. The reason for the one-on-one was for a fighter to talk to the sport's biggest detractor, a meeting of the minds where Brian, a likeable baby-faced jiu-jitsu specialist and experienced New York-based fighter stuck fighting pro shows in New Jersey, could educate the uneducated. Brian's uncle knew the legislator from other projects, and knew that Assemblyman Reilly was MMA's public enemy number one, so a meeting between the legislator and the fighter was on like Donkey Kong.

I liked Brian, and as with many his threads intertwined and crisscrossed with all the usual suspects: though a jiu-jitsu ace, he'd honed his striking with the ringers at Tiger Schulmann; he had fought a friend named Carmine at a sanctioned show in New Jersey; and when he brought his students to compete at an underground show in Upstate New York called Bike 'N' Brawl, he didn't withhold details when he told me about the experience ("I'll say this for the promoters: they're trying").

I asked about Assemblyman Reilly's misgivings. Brian took a deep breath, an unspoken "Where do I begin?" prefacing what came next. "He felt that it would be kind of sending the wrong message to the youth of America. He actually equated mixed martial arts violence to gang violence at one point. Our conversation was shockingly civil, but this was the one thing I kind of got upset at. I said to him, 'I've had a lot of hard times in my life where, if anything, mixed martial arts kept me on the right path.' I've been doing mixed martial arts since I was fifteen, and I was having a lot of problems with my parents. One of the reasons I didn't do anything criminal or get too out of line was that I had something to lose. If I did that, I wouldn't be able to train jiu-jitsu. And I talked about how I have people every day at my school who train with me, and I'll hear from their families how they're a better father now, or a better brother now, or a better son, or they'll get better grades in school.

"One of the last things he said was, 'Would you let your kid go to a mixed martial arts event?' I told him a lot of students bring their young children to the events. I have no problem with that. I would rather my child take mixed martial arts classes than take peewee football. It would be safer for him and I think he'd learn better life lessons. He was kind of surprised to hear that.

"What I was trying to make clear to him was, whether he sanctions mixed martial arts or not, it's going to occur," Brian said. "It's either going to occur in things like the Underground Combat League or the Bike 'N' Brawl or other events. It's going to happen. Which would you rather? Would you rather it happen in a sanctioned, overseen professional event? Or would you rather it happen on the fly, in a place that might have insufficient facilities—rings might break, they could have staph on the mat, or they don't have the proper medical personnel? He said, 'Have you ever seen them tell a fighter that he couldn't fight because something had happened in the ring?' And I said yes, that was something that had happened to me in my last fight [on *The Ultimate Fighter*]. I was hit with an illegal blow, immediately a doctor was called in and asked to make a determination if I should continue fighting. They said that I couldn't. And I was taken to the hospital and given a CT scan, and that was regardless of if I had wanted to or not. Trust me, if I could have gotten away with not going to the hospital, I wouldn't have gone. This wasn't a choice I had, this was something the [Nevada] athletic commission did on their own accord for the safety of the fighters, and they said I couldn't fight for six months. In six weeks my nose was healed. Easily. But they did that, and they made sure, because they didn't want a tragedy to occur. If anything, they were overprotective. And I think he was impressed by that. He wasn't aware of all the oversight that occurs."

What of the issue of unsanctioned, underground shows that occur throughout New York State now? "I told him how in New Jersey you don't have these underground shows. I never get invited to an underground show in New Jersey. I get invited to them all the time in New York."

The issue of safety—that oldie but goodie—of course

arose. "He actually thought you couldn't grab a guy and hit him because it's not safe, that combining those two arts was too dangerous," said Brian. "I had to explain to him that in original boxing rules you could do that. Then boxing evolved. And he said, 'Well, that's because it was too unsafe,' and I said no, it was done for spectator reasons. That's why they took the grappling out of boxing. He couldn't deal with the fact that someone could be on the ground, seemingly helpless, and be struck. He said that his constituents come up to him every day and talk about how that offends them and their morality, and that leads him to think that it has to be banned. He really thinks he's doing the noble fight with this."

It's not until June 2009 that the issue again hit the Committee on Tourism, Arts, and Sports Development's docket, and when it did all eyes were upon the promised fisticuff between Assemblyman Reilly and those pushing toward legalizing mixed martial arts. True to form, Assemblyman Reilly did his best, decrying violence and even showing a clip of UFC champions Brock Lesnar and Randy Couture pounding the bejeesus out of each other. The assembled legislators cast their votes. Fourteen were for the bill, six against. An unrelated coup in the Senate would kill the process that year, and a lame duck governor would stymie it the next, but it was a just a matter of time.

III

Not long after Sammy's Martial Arts Madness extravaganza I was contacted by Jerry, who informed me of a show he was helping put together out on Long Island, at the Funaro twins' gym in the town of Patchogue.

Snapshot of the Funaro twins, James and Joe: watch

enough MMA and the mediocre fighters all blend together into some half-assed, half-caring meta-fighter, but the truly talented—the ones who take that talent and mold it with hard work and sweat until they're a keener and keener edge every time you see them—will always stick out. James was one such fighter. I first saw James fight at a UCL in Queens, and he ended up a repeat customer, serving up stud-level grappling and sharp striking to whoever wanted some. He lost quickly to Josh the ex-Marine, but James returned, and when he took on Kirkland the wrestler at a UCL in upper Manhattan, he knocked Kirkland out with a kick to the head, a kick with the kind of flair and panache that would've made the ghost of Bruce Lee say, "Dude, nicely done." James had sampled life in the world of sanctioned MMA, in New Jersey, Ohio, and Pennsylvania, but unsanctioned fighting was his current scene—for now, at least.

Though there were eleven fights between them and James possessed the lion's share, Joe was cut from the same cloth. As twins, both were carbon copies of the same pale, in-shape, and frequently smirking stereotype, unassuming and unintimidating until they stripped down to their fight shorts and started kicking your ass. (James would later confess to me that he sometimes went to bars looking for fights, acting like a meek victim-in-waiting until someone mistook him for easy prey.)

On a rainy Saturday night I made the trek, navigating the Long Island Expressway until I was at the venue. It was a full-service gym on the far end of Main Street, the bottom floor an expansive room packed with a variety of weights and exercise equipment, the top floor equipped with mats and a boxing ring, and now, for this "Patchogue Fight Night," rows of folding chairs. The audience skewed young but there were

older people there, too, parents and family members of fighters, and each time James Funaro took the microphone and
addressed the crowd, he made a point of saying how the
event was being held for charity and that the proceeds were
going toward some stricken kid's medical bills. Jerry scurried
about, a busy beaver gathering up competitors like sticks and
competently building a dam, and after a while I gleaned from
him what the card would look like—a pair of preteens in
headgear doing a boxing match, some grappling, and the *piece
de resistance*: a full-fledged MMA bout starring Joe Funaro and
an athletic black boxer from Brooklyn named Rashad.

I asked James what he had been up to. Other than a
couple of underground fights at a school with a cage (a cage
was a rarity, although less so now that MMA had redefined
the martial arts instruction industry) just outside of New York
City many months ago, James had otherwise kept clean, holding firm to his desire to turn pro and somewhat discouraged
that the New Jersey pro leagues wouldn't return his phone
calls.

At my question, James shook his head. He may have been
the possessor of a warrior's skills, refined and sharpened and
greater than those most men ever attain, but he was still a
twenty-two-year-old wiseass, and trouble finds twenty-two-
year-old wiseasses if those twenty-two-year-old wiseasses
don't find it first. "It's such bullshit," James said, and began
his tale. Weeks before he had gone from martial arts school
to martial arts school handing out flyers for a grappling tournament, inviting anyone interested, and one traditional karate
instructor in particular took great umbrage at James's visit,
even going so far as to grab James and throw him up against
a wall. But a flurry of punches to the face and the karate
instructor had had enough, and the two shook hands and

agreed that the matter was done and best forgotten. But it wasn't. Soon James was notified that he had a temporary restraining order against him, and after that the police showed up, claiming he had violated the TRO by calling the karate instructor and leaving threatening messages on his voice mail. According to James, even the police agreed the whole thing was bogus, but procedures were procedures, and James had had to spend the night in jail.

"I never called him," he said to me. "It was probably one of his students. My lawyer says I just have to get the phone records to prove I didn't make the call."

Peter was there at Patchogue Fight Night, acting as a judge, and I saddled up next to him in the cramped area beside the ring. He pulled out his phone and showed me a picture of him and Kimbo Slice—Kimbo a former back-yard fighter-turned-MMA superstar—having dinner the night before at an Upper East Side restaurant. The most popular unsanctioned fighter of all time was now a competitor on *The Ultimate Fighter* and in New York as part of a whirlwind media tour to promote the SpikeTV show. Peter knew Kimbo from a straight-to-DVD film they had worked on together, *Blood and Bone*, Kimbo playing a prison denizen and Peter inexplicably a referee for an underground fight, and Peter described how much Kimbo stuck out in the fancy restaurant, and that stuffy, old white women had approached the massive and imposing black man for his autograph.

The venue was packed and the crowd was alive, cheering on each fight, mothers applauding and fathers pumping their fists in the air when a punch landed clean, or when a fighter hoisted another in the air and dropped him, or when someone snagged a submission. You could see a million pay-per-views on television and soak in the noise of countless anonymous fans at a massive arena-sized live show, but nothing beats the fervor of those with a stake in the fight, those family members rooting for their beloved sons and cousins and siblings and nephews, made crazy by the dance of violence. The gym could barely contain the bedlam. Just a few bouts in and the windows had steamed up and the atmosphere was thick with sweat and exertion, dank with the kind of odor anxiousness and excitement put off, and a glance outside, at the warm autumn night and the wet streets, offered only the illusion of catching a breath of fresh air.

And then it was the main event, and Joe entered the ring to take on Rashad of the Brooklyn Fight Factory, which was really just the name of a group of guys who trained together, sometimes at coach Rage Rivas's place, sometimes at the gym at Hunter College in Manhattan. Thin and in-shape Rashad and stocky, agreeable Hispanic Rage were newcomers to the scene, fresh faces, welcomed as unknown variables willing to fight, and when Rashad and Joe engaged it was clear that, though green in regard to the whole grappling thing, Rashad had enough boxing skill and natural athleticism to be dangerous. Joe stood and traded for a bit and went for the takedown, putting Rashad on the canvas but unable to capitalize, and now there was a cut, nasty and angry, trickling blood out and over the Funaro twin's eye. The referee stood them up, examined the gash, and said, "You can go until the end of the round but I'm stopping it then." Joe's desperation was almost palpable and he tried once more on the ground and a few times on the feet, probing for a submission and pawing with his punches. Rashad did not, however, make a mistake, and when time ran out in the first and only round, the ref signaled that it was all over. Rookie Rashad's hand was raised and he was declared the winner.

Joe had a towel pressed to his head, applying direct pressure on his brand-spanking-new battle scar. He would need stitches and someone to cover for him tomorrow at his job at the Olive Garden. As Rashad and Rage celebrated, I could almost hear a licking of chops, James and Joe wanting revenge and Peter wanting whatever potential scrappers the Brooklyn Fight Factory had to offer. I congratulated Rashad and told Joe it was a good fight. Joe had a line of friends patting him on the back, and from around the towel he looked at me almost apologetically, as if he had done something erroneous or improper by losing. But he had it wrong, he had fought hard and had entertained, and I, too, patted him on the back.

October 2009, and I was at the Jacob Javits Center on the west side of Manhattan, a cavernous complex where New Yorkers come for auto and boat shows, comic book conventions, to sit for the State Bar Exam, or, for this weekend, to visit something called the World MMA Expo. There were booths set up, vendors selling gear and T-shirts and a variety of supplements promising weight loss and muscle gain and superpowers, each booth manned by a stereotypical hard ass (goatee, tribal tattoos, arms in a constant state of flex; you know a sport has made it when its followers have their own stereotype), and one or two young beauties in undersized clothes. Within a cage near the entrance some UFC fighters wielded pens—Wanderlei Silva, Matt Hughes, Pete Sell, Phillipe Nover, Pete Spratt—doling out autographs to a line of fans at least a hundred deep, and on a mat at the far end of the combative sports bazaar, masters of jiu-jitsu, Muay Thai, and boxing gave brief, ten-minute lessons to a mass of eyes and clicking digital cameras.

I was in a conference room, for the panel discussion titled

"The Future of MMA in New York," chewing the fat before it began, talking with Melvina, Eddie Goldman, and Mike Kim, the young lawyer who drafted the current version of the bill that would legalize the sport in the Empire State. Melvina told me of how close, how very close the bill came to getting passed, that she was instructed days before to make her way up to Albany for the signing and to help iron out the specifics, and that when the State Senate crapped the bed she was called that very morning and told not to come. (I was told a similar story by Jeff Blatnick, an Olympic Gold Medalist wrestler and early UFC commentator. As a New Yorker, Jeff had worked tirelessly to get the sport legalized, and he, too, was going to Albany that day and was then informed not to bother, that it wasn't happening.) Eddie, knowledgeable and eccentric Eddie, talked of MMA's history as the oft-persecuted innocent, while Mike said that the legalization process would start up again in January, when the next legislative session began. According to Mike, the bill would have to go back to square one, in the Assembly committee where it had first encountered problems, but that it shouldn't meet any resistance, the dissenters having shot their collective wad the first time around.

Day two of the panel discussion and Melvina was gone and I was in her place, the resident expert on underground shows. In the days leading up to the bill's supposed final leg of its journey to actual law, Peter had texted me asking for updates on its status, and when everything went off the rails I had let him know that he had more time. Peter said that he would go legitimate if he had to, if the folks at the New York State Athletic Commission were on the up and up and worth working with, but who knows? Maybe, with sanctioned pro shows and approved amateur leagues around, the UCL would go quietly into the night. Or maybe the UCL would never die, a great, immortal *vale tudo* party shared by a select few. But it was a moot discussion until the bill was passed, and it's impossible to count the sands in the top half of an hourglass.

You only know that time is running out.

PETER

The images conjured whenever you tell someone about the underground show, the questions raised and whispered, like the New Jersey commission official at a Newark event who leaned in and with awe in his voice asked, "Is it like the movies?" And always the answer is a grin, a half shrug, and a "Sure, sometimes." Because the truth never strayed too far from fiction, to what the imagination dreamed up. Like, of course it doesn't even remotely resemble a sanctioned affair, and of course people have been plucked from the audience to compete—what else would you expect? "It's just life imitating art," Peter once told me, and like his UCL—chock full of stereotypes and some of them true—so, too, is the man behind it.

Oh, the mosaic of facts that go into a person, the sum of something I know for years before the individual parts are revealed, and when he tells me them, the pieces to a human puzzle fall into place. Spofford Juvenile Detention Center after stabbing his uncle. Rikers Island after beating up his father ("He was a crackhead," he tells me). Somewhere in there is judo, getting kicked out of a prominent club because "they didn't like my attitude." A brief marriage ending ugly. Subtle and not-so-subtle promises of violence—to rivals, to unkind journalists, to those who threaten the sanctity of his UCL baby. I've witnessed Peter smooth-talk, beg, and coax people into getting in the ring as much as him pour on the disgust and impugn their manhood when they wouldn't. There's been elation on his face, a sense of accomplishment when an event rattled off nine bouts and everyone present was sated, and there's been demoralization and embarrassment, when despite his best efforts only three bouts came together. What affected him more? Taking a beating in the ring before a hundred spectators or the news that a deranged busboy murdered some girl at a nightclub where Peter had worked the door? (Answer: the latter.) I've seen him charge people at the door and barely break even, and I've seen him foot the bill for the space and let in only a few spectators, gratis. So many facets. You think going in that the promoter of an underground fight show is going to be smoking a cigar and radiate the kind of vibe that makes you want to shower after being in his presence, but the reality of it is, he's maybe some of the things you'd think, maybe none.

Get to know Peter and he's funny, amiable even, but before you cross that threshold he's an enigma with a goatee, receding hairline, pensive eyes, and a Bronx native's sometimes smooth, sometimes coarse manner of speaking. There's desire and drive there, the gift of gab and a quiet demeanor that can be perceived as either a willingness to shake your hand or stab you if the need arises. And yet the 180-pound Latino's most telling asset is his readiness to get into the ring, to scrap, to give customers another bout to hoot and holler for. At an early event in Manhattan, Peter issued an appeal to the audience for someone, anyone, interested in fighting him, and at another UCL edition in the Bronx he capped off the night with a battle that left his white judo uniform a bloody tie-dye of carnage. When I asked him why he fought, he told me, "I fight because it's something I've always done, so it's natural for me. But more importantly, because I want to test my judo skills. That's really it, for the sake of testing my judo skills." (That question comes early on; years later I wonder if his fighting has taken on a kind of inertia of its own, like the grizzled veteran who somehow can't say "no" when the ring beckons.)

The mosaic of facts, told to me when we're walking out of his gym, told to me when he's sitting at the dinner table at my home, a big bowl of pasta between him, my wife, and myself, and yet no tableau is complete without looking at the works the man has put forth. Some see insight into Ansel Adams or Vincent van Gogh or Frank Lloyd Wright by analyzing their creations; the same can be said of Peter and his show, and the lives that have been touched.

After watching Chris the first few times I was left with the impression that he wasn't cut out for this sort of thing. He was short with a big potbelly attached to his small frame, and though eager and willing, he was a 175-pound fighter who should've been competing with opponents who weighed forty pounds less, people who would be his own size if he lost the excess baggage. At a UCL in the Bronx in 2007, Chris stepped into the ring to face a personal trainer and aspiring actor named Mike, chiseled Mike, Mike whose agent told him this was a casting call and who didn't flinch when Peter told him that no, this was for an actual underground fight, and when Chris and Mike squared off it was the epitome of mismatch. Weighing 170 pounds, Mike was in peak physical condition and looked like he could be posing for headshots; Chris was shorter and heavier, a little guy lugging around a spare

tire. And it was ugly, as these one-sided things often are. Pro-
ducers for *The Iron Ring*, an MMA reality show on the BET
network, sat in the stands scouting for potential contestants,
and they looked the other way when Chris eventually told
the referee that he was giving up. Chris was so disgusted with
himself he bolted, claiming he was done with MMA, not even
waiting around for his New Generation Karate teammates,
and when they told me his nickname was "Psycho" I thought
of how it fit.

But he returned for the next show, this time at Steve
Katz's school in Queens. Chris's teammates were studs, like
Josh the ex-Marine and Lance the mortician (Lance usually
showed up to these things in a suit, fresh from "the office."
The running joke was that there was a body lying in a coffin
in the back of the hearse parked outside, and there probably
was.) Still, Chris had a ways to go, and after a long battle his
opponent tapped him out with a triangle choke. Elsewhere on
the card Harley Flanagan, the lead singer of the hardcore
group The Cro-Mags, popped his MMA cherry and lost to a
young, mellow-looking kid named Marwin, and when the
underground promotion returned to the Bronx, Marwin took
on Chris. Chris bowed before the match began and fought
hard, harder than I had ever seen him fight before, and
though the Renzo Gracie-trained Marwin stayed one step
ahead, enough of Chris was on display to discern some in-
fight traits. He was impossibly kind and respectful even in
the midst of battle, at one point visibly contemplating stomp-
ing on Marwin's face (a legal move in *vale tudo*) to escape a
submission but instead holding back. Again Chris lost, a tap
out when the armbar he was caught in became indefensible,
and after congratulating his foe, he fled the ring furious.
When I made my way to the locker room to tell him he had a

good fight, Chris screamed at me to leave him alone and pounded on a locker for emphasis. Josh and Lance gave me apologetic looks as I turned to go.

A year passed and it was time for Peter's latest, this one at a boxing gym across the street from a ramshackle, abandoned building in Brooklyn, and when I walked in, the Chris I saw was someone I barely recognized. Gone was the fat. Gone was the anger. He was 133 pounds and full of confidence, the kind of confidence only consistent and dedicated training could bring, and now, with his hair buzzed short and a tuft of fuzz on his chin, his grin seemed genuine and full of depth. Like yes, he had found that peace that had eluded him, found it within the confines of hard work and training, and he was truly happy.

The audience was sparse for this UCL installment, but there was action in the ring nonetheless. Muscular forty-eight-year-old ex-Army Ranger Kevin had a rematch with a chubby Hispanic he had wrecked in the Bronx, and he beat him worse than before, the chubby Hispanic needing almost an eternity to regain his senses and exit the ring ("He's done in the UCL," Peter said later of the fighter, whose three trips into underground combat had ended with three quick and ugly losses). Two others went at it, a wrestler from Long Island and a bulky older guy who was no stranger to needles, and when things started to go poorly for him, the older guy used a takedown attempt as an excuse to fall through the ropes and feign an injury. An Ultimate Karate student who looked like he meant business dispensed a beating, and in another bout a pale and scrawny Irish teenager swung wildly and got knocked out, his coach and Jerry (acting as referee) at his side instantly and attending to his prone form as the kid stared breathlessly up at the ceiling. James was there, again as an announcer, and Rashad was absent, and when I approached Rage and inquired about him, I was told Rashad was sitting this one out.

And then it was Chris's turn, his opponent a diminutive fighter from Brooklyn nicknamed Lionheart, short and thin, with a shaved head and in amazing shape, as if an ancient Greek statue and a "Bodies" exhibit model had gotten married and produced a son who grew up to participate in underground fights. Chris shook Lionheart's hand when Jerry called them both to the center, shook his hand warmly with both of his own and bowed his head, and that moment of niceness was a stark contrast to the nonstop assault that followed. For all three rounds Chris was flawless, zigging when Lionheart zagged, taking him down and securing every dominant position in the book (those positions can vary depending on the book, but you can't argue when one man spends the entire time attacking and the other does nothing but defends). The tap out never came—Lionheart was skilled and knew what he was doing enough to escape—but it was a great fight, made greater by Chris's team chanting "Psycho! Psycho! Psycho!" and the formerly overweight, ill-tempered New Generation Karate fighter's complete and total rebirth in the ring. There was no question Chris had earned the decision when time ran out, and afterward he and Lionheart hung out and laughed, like two best friends catching up on old times even though they'd just met.

There are success stories in the underground, like UFC fighter Frankie and others who graduated to the pro leagues and made names for themselves, and there are the sad stories, like Lamont Tareyton Williams, and there are more who fell by the wayside, never to be heard from again. Chris's was a success story, a Cinderella tale if there ever was one, and if

MMA had never taken hold and grown viable in the Empire State—and to a lesser extent, if the UCL had never existed— would this fighter at heart have ever had cause to transform from caterpillar to badass butterfly?

His New Generation Karate and American Freestyle team was progressive, firmly held within the grasp of Muay Thai and Brazilian Jiu-Jitsu effectiveness, and when not working for an airline and watching anime, Chris ate, drank, and slept fighting. "'Psycho' was a nickname given to me by American Freestyle trainer Rudy Luna," he said. "When I started train- ing with him I was about five feet even and 170 pounds of fat-boy. I think it was a combination of being completely unafraid or too stupid to be afraid, as well as not tapping (even when I should have—I don't think at the time I even knew what 'tap' meant). It led to Rudy yelling, 'What are you? Psycho?' And after that, the name just stuck."

Chris described his first MMA fight, a losing battle at an event in Massachusetts where he had won over the crowd with his no-quit attitude and gameness, and I asked what made him want to compete. "It came very natural to me," he said. "When I was younger, I was very small and always picked on. I guess in an effort to prove that I wasn't just some little guy to push around anymore, I decided to fight, just for the experience and to see what would happen. Also, it's a world that I understand. You don't get ahead because of who you know or brown-nosing; you get ahead, or fail, because of what you put in—how hard you train, how hard you work, and how hungry you are. My life turned itself around through my training with Rudy and the American Freestyle team."

I thought about how most fighters have to get into the "zone" when they fight, as if a switch must be turned on and

off to inflict violence, and that Chris, no matter what tran-
spired, was perhaps one of the nicest people you could ever
brawl with. He laughed when I asked him about it.

"While I'm not sure if it's a good or bad part of the way I
fight, I'm quite sure there's no switch," he said. "In general, I
don't tend to be a very emotional person. I do get angry from
time to time, but when I'm angry, I don't channel it into a
fight—unless it's warranted, i.e., someone hits a woman in
front of me. I have no zone. If I did, then I'm always in it. [In
a fight,] I don't feel as if I'm being nice, or cruel. I put the necessary force into a fight. I'm not going to smash somebody's
head open unless I have to, and if I can beat my opponent
without needing to, I will. However, as cold as it may sound,
the same is true for the other side of the fence. If I have to
draw blood, or break a bone, I will do that.

"I love to fight, and fight hard, and I'm one of the few
people who, in his past, has had to fight literally just to stay
alive. These days it's too much about hatred and anger, but
not for me. I want to have great fights, with great people.
Smile, laugh, joke, punch, kick, bleed, and still be able to
shake the man's hand when it's over.

"I would love to fight in a sanctioned show, invite my
friends, etcetera," Chris said to me. "But at the same time, if
there are ridiculously watered-down rules, I wouldn't want
to waste my time. I don't want to fight with my hands tied
behind my back." Did that rule out New Jersey's amateur
shows, which are laden with an assortment of rules and
restrictions? "From what I have seen and from what I have
heard, the amateur shows in Jersey are relatively weak. They
are more like glorified sparring matches rather than fights. I
feel like it's a waste of time. You want to fight, then you have
to fight. No attacks to the head on the ground and no kicks to

head standing even with shin pads? Yeah, those fighters are such badasses, really putting themselves on the line. Those types of leagues are only for those who either: a) can't fight, b) are scared of a real fight, or c) just want their fifteen minutes in the spotlight. I mean, they do help put MMA on the map, and I'm sure they are good for a younger generation of fighters, but those who intend to fly high should steer clear."

And what of Peter's UCL? "The UCL, aside from being a local show that makes competing close to home easy and much more accessible, is a 'no bullshit' league. It's more open, everyone knows everyone in the league. In most large-scale, commercial leagues, such as the UFC, it's business-driven. It's about making money and talking trash. The more trash a fighter talks, the more money he makes. That's simply not what I'm about. I like the tight-knit feel. And while the fighters are tough, vicious, and competitive, not once in the UCL did I ever encounter a single trash-talker, or anything other than real and true camaraderie and sportsmanship. Just a higher class of people. The UCL is a place you compete for you, not for a career or a camera." Added this underground success story, "It's where real fighters come to fight."

Where real fighters come to fight, and where aspiring fighters learn what it really means to know how to fight, chasing the answer to the question "What works?" The sport is all about that ever-present thrill, but for every person taking part in it for a helping of adrenaline there are those engaged in mixed martial arts for reasons bordering on the scientific. In Ancient Rome, gladiators en route to the sandy arena floor were given exotic weapons like a net and a three-pronged trident or some other deadly accoutrement one would never find on an actual battlefield. Maybe it had something to do with raw entertainment, but it definitely tapped into the imagination, definitely raised eyebrows and piqued the collective pugilistic curiosity. Human toys laid out in miniature wars, the combination of violent possibilities taking fascination to near-limitless heights, and it has permeated mixed martial arts at every level.

Before the UFC, there really wasn't much in terms of empirical evidence as to what worked and what didn't in unarmed combat. Bruce Lee and *The Karate Kid* made punching and kicking and esoteric things like katas and board-breaking popular, professional wrestlers were in their own world of choreographed moves, and no one gave a damn about what was going on in judo tournaments or at high school wrestling meets. But in Brazil *vale tudo* was like boxing in that it could be a ticket out of the ghetto, and Japan has always had a hankering for all things *budo*, so when 1993 came and the Ultimate Fighting Championship gave Americans a chance to see a scrawny Brazilian named Royce Gracie use leverage and technique to break arms and choke foes unconscious, there were fighters out there who actually had a firm grasp on what it really meant to know how to fight. Or they were damn close to the formula. And given time, that formula—written out on some grand celestial chalkboard—changed, with variables and factors and whole sections erased and altered and retooled.

Seeing it all play out on the international stage, with Brazilians dominating and then losing consistently to wrestlers wise to their tricks, and then with the age of cross-trained athletes emerging, and watching it play out in similar fashion on the regional shows and the tiniest underground affairs like trickle-down economics cash reaching the lower class, data culled from those varied perspectives could flesh out quite a few thesis papers and dissertations. Still, there were some who seemed like they never got the memo, and the stories of their failure are sometimes just as intriguing as the stories of the victors.

Promoter Lou Neglia's Ring of Combat has been the pinnacle of East Coast regional promotions since 2002, with the best fighters going from Ring of Combat in New Jersey to the UFC in a manner similar to minor league baseball teams feeding the major league its most worthy. Careers are made at Ring of Combat. Fighters shine. Or fighters shatter.

Enter Gregor and Igor Gracie, brothers from Rio de Janeiro living in New York and teaching at Renzo Gracie's Manhattan academy. Brazilian expats rotate in and out of that academy like it's a semester abroad program, albeit one that involves teaching the most effective ways to torque shoulders and knee joints and choke people unconscious, and Gregor and Igor were the newest generation of jiu-jitsu royalty and every bit the grappling masters their namesake implies. At Ring of Combat 18, at the Tropicana Casino & Resort in Atlantic City, Gregor and Igor took on two very experienced fighters in Doug and Tom. On paper, comparing the Gracies' grappling accomplishments to Doug's and Tom's checkered MMA records, it looked as if the two Americans were going to step into the ring and be forced to tap out before the timekeeper even had a chance to start his stopwatch. But it takes a special kind of hubris to assume all you need nowadays is a black belt in jiu-jitsu and to assume that because your name is Gracie and your opponent has only a purple belt (a full two levels lower than your black belt), that you'd wipe the mats with him in training and how can it be any different in a fight? Or that you don't need to work on your cardio because you'll tap your opponent out before you can work up a sweat,

and why bother working on wrestling or boxing or kickboxing (all of which are essential for success, or even survival)
for this, your third (for Gregor) and first (for Igor) fight? Uncle
Renzo, beloved by all, may be a legend and a pioneer in the
sport, but that aforementioned memo on what works and
what doesn't, yeah, Gregor and Igor seemed to have ignored
it. Things like that get you on the wrong end of a highlight
reel. Things like that guarantee you the kind of beating
reserved for prison-bound pedophiles and a spot in history
as The Guy Who Got Knocked the Fuck Out on Live Television. Things like that ensure that your cousin, Kyra Gracie,
is going to weep in her seat in the bleachers as they try to
revive you, and when you're at the academy, sure, your students will pat you on the back and say, "Good effort." But
what they really mean is, "Damn! You took that shin right to
the face!"

Doug, a bald, black-skinned family man, and Tom, a part-
time college student and part-time DJ missing a front tooth,
did get the memo and they read it closely, following its
instructions like newfound Bible thumpers scrutinizing scrip-
ture. They could do everything the Gracies could not, i.e.,
wrestle and throw strikes, and they had the conditioning to
go all three five-minute rounds at full speed. In the UFC, men
like Forrest Griffin and Randy Couture can fight and win
wherever the action ends up, and further down the ladder, on
the rung dominated by Ring of Combat and on the rung
where the UCL rests, that little tidbit known as cross-training
is gaining veracity every single day two fighters of varying
backgrounds strap on four-ounce gloves and throw down.
You either know how to do it all—throw a decent punch or
kick, shoot a decent takedown or prevent one, slap on a choke
or armlock or know how to avoid them—or you don't, and if

you don't, you'll be bowing your head when the announcer calls out your opponent's name and the referee raises the hand of the man who just beat you high in the air.

Lessons learned, in the Octagon and broadcast on pay-per-view, at a Ring of Combat before a crowd of two thousand, and in the UCL's microcosm of knuckles-to-the-chops reality, a small slice of the pie that is the laboratory of true unarmed fighting but a slice nonetheless. Maybe Gregor and Igor would've dominated if they'd ventured into the UCL, maybe they would've been tested, maybe they would've learned something that could've helped them. We'll never know. But the classroom was there, just waiting for pupils to take their chairs and gaze upon the chalkboard. (Igor got back on the horse a few months later and performed up to expectations, and though it would be two and a half years before Gregor returned to the cage, when he did fight he looked every bit the seasoned pro.)

July of 2008, and the first thing I notice when I walk into the boxing gym is the man in the fedora with the camera on his shoulder and the blond reporter beside him, recognizable to anyone possessing even a cursory acquaintance with local TV, holding a microphone with "Fox 5 News" emblazoned on its side. The two huddle together like clean-cut white missionaries unsure if the natives are going to accept their Christian teachings or cook them in a pot full of carrots, celery, and water, and just as when the *New York Times* sent a photographer, when *Newsday* sent a correspondent, or when Channel 9 had someone doing post-fight interviews ringside, their presence adds an air of legitimacy to the proceedings. You can argue about a tree that falls in the woods making no noise when no one is around to hear it, but when mainstream press shows up at an underground show, you'll have a tough time denying that that fight where the transit worker nearly lost an eye and where the dentist nearly lost his teeth actually happened. Credibility goes up, while deniability goes down.

The students appear in the classroom, some individually, others in groups. There's Shawn, the hard-hitting Wing Chun stylist practicing his grappling; Chaz, the aforementioned New York City transit worker, trained by Peter; Josh the ex-Marine, a State Farm insurance rep during the week and ass-kicker on the weekends; Kirkland the wrestler, quiet as usual; and a team of young and eagers from a martial arts club at Baruch College, ready to see if all their hard work will result in passing grades.

My pre-show wander takes me upstairs to where the Baruch College boys are warming up, hitting pads with their Asian trainer and pausing to stare into the camera and speak into the *Fox 5 News* reporter's microphone. There's Robert the Dentist, slated for the main event against Josh, and Chaz's opponent, John, plus little Gabriel and Julio, bright-eyed and bushy-tailed, nervous with anticipation. In a room across the hall Josh is getting his hands wrapped, in another, light-blue T-shirts with the word *Warriors* on them are being handed out and donned in unison, the private Chaz army.

Downstairs and the floorboards creak wildly as over a hundred spectators file in, the occasional fist smacking idly into a nearby dangling duct-taped heavy bag as the bleachers are filled and many are forced to claim a spot somewhere standing. Out the back door a few are smoking cigarettes, someone even lights up a joint, and Chris is before the camera now and asked why he fights. A year away from his rebirth and he spews bravado, dropping gems like "you have something to say to me, say it in the ring," and the reporter eats it up, eats up the thickness of the crowd and the energy of the room—an energy that increases a thousandfold once the fights are underway.

Shawn the Wing Chun stylist out-grapples a hefty jiu-jitsu guy, twisting an arm for the tap out, and Kirkland dumps his foe onto the canvas and finds the same finishing move for himself. Gabriel calls it quits on his stool, too spent from the frantic back-and-forth of the first round of his fight to go on, and his teammate Julio succumbs to a choke. By the time Chris and Marwin have at it, the crowd is near frenzied, and the reporter is doing her best to make sure her cameraman has a clear, up-close, and personal view. (No one objects; everyone scoots aside to make room for him ringside.)

And then it's Chaz and John's turn, each making their way down the stairs and to the ring, the sea of bodies parting for their entrances and applause greeting them as they step through the ropes. Peter's in Chaz's corner, wearing a light-blue Warriors T-shirt, and John stares across at them, his own team issuing forth bursts of instruction and encouragement too dense to decipher. The referee, a New Jersey pro fighter named Andrew, calls them to the center for a touch of the gloves, and after gesturing for them to move back, nods at the timekeeper (just someone with a watch with a second timer) and shouts for them to fight.

At 176 pounds John has a seven-pound weight advantage, and being a few inches taller and wiry gives him the benefit of a slightly longer reach, so when Chaz wades in to throw leather John's already clipped him once, twice, and they're kicking, and punching, and tying up, and when they tumble to the canvas they're punching some more and angling for a submission that could end it all. Chaz is getting the worst of it, and when Round One expires he stands and all can see his eye: grotesque, horrific, swollen shut.

The Baruch College boys have thus far seen two of their clan lose, but the "W" here is so close they can taste it, and it makes them frantic with elation. Andrew's standing before Chaz, looking into the MTA worker's face, shaking his head and saying he wants to call the bout, but Chaz begs him not to and he's joined by Peter. The cameraman stands on the ring apron and gets a close up. Ultimately, the choice lies with the referee, and when Andrew finally says that the bout can go on—despite a fighter with clearly one functional eye—the crowd claps heartily. Everyone who came to see action, everyone who came to see what works and what doesn't, they're all getting what they came for, but they're also witnesses to the bonus lesson of bonus lessons. They're glimpsing firsthand the purest expression of fighting heart, and that makes them lean forward, crane their necks, or even leave their seats and push closer.

Andrew says "go" and Chaz and John stride forward, Chaz covering his blind side and trying to keep his head a moving, elusive target. John finds him, though, with a jab, with a kick, with a knee, and soon the smaller man is forced to jump up and wrap his legs around his opponent, allowing gravity to pull John down on top of him. They struggle, a deft shift of weight here and a well-timed swivel there, and Chaz has swept John and is on top. The crowd is a frenzy of screams and cheers and clapping. Chaz, one eye swollen shut but obviously unbreakable, attempts a choke, and when John pushes him away, the bus mechanic grabs his arm and moves to hyperextend it. John taps out.

Chaz is the winner.

The Baruch College boys are crushed. Meanwhile, the ring

is flooded with light-blue T-shirts, including Peter and any number of friends, and Chaz is so full of emotion all he can do is flex and scream "Warriors!" at the cameraman. Outside the ring, utter pandemonium. Right at this very moment, at this point in time and forever in the memory of all who are there to have seen it, Chaz is a superstar.

Lessons learned, and when things calm down and Josh enters the ring to take on Robert the Dentist, the beatdown that follows is almost academic. Andrew bellows for them to begin and Robert walks into a right hand that smashes his nose. Seconds later Josh is on Robert's back, and with blood leaking everywhere Robert is tapping out to a tight choke. Four fighters and four losses, and one of the Baruch College boys' groupies—a young, tall Asian kid—is on the verge of tears. But that's how it goes, and a year later Robert wins an amateur bout at a sanctioned show at the Mohegan Sun Casino in Connecticut, so what transpires this Sunday night in July at the UCL isn't for naught.

(Weeks later the *Fox 5 News* piece airs, heavy on the sensationalism and brutality, short on the footage of a post-fight Chaz embracing John and shaking the hands of his teammates, the Baruch College boys hugging him back and each thanking the other. Also missing is Josh talking about the discipline and devotion required to fight. To anyone watching, the UCL is just a den of bloodthirsty villains.)

"Few rules, but to the fighters, pure sport," said the *New York Times* article on the unsanctioned league, and that notion has made the promotion a flame irresistible to the moths of combat, to nearly every shade of testosterone-driven throwback to the war-less warriors of old. And yet for every street fighter who wanders in looking to test himself, there's a well-trained athlete, for every rube, a state wrestling champ or Golden Gloves boxer, for every Five Animal Kung Fu stylist, a legitimate cross-trained striker/grappler, for every one-hit wonder, a stud in the making.

It's December, and James Funaro is scheduled to step into the cage at a legit, fully sanctioned fight show across the Hudson in New Jersey. There, the sport is legal and packed with rules and restrictions, a different beast entirely, and to Peter it's about as close to actual fighting as a five-dollar lap dance is to sex. James will be facing Mike Fischetti, a fighter from one of the Tiger Schulmann chain of martial arts schools, a by-the-book dojo and the opposite side of the underground coin, its representatives and their haunts the antithesis of kicking ass in secret, unsanctioned events. I ask Peter for a prediction and there's no hesitation.

"James by any way he wants it," he says. Through the years Peter's underground circuit has swallowed up everything from trained athletes and martial artists to street fighters and miscreants, spitting out the talentless, the unfocused, the disillusioned and churning out a few, a select few, with a genuine future. The 175-pound James can knock out a charging wrestler with a precise, exact kick to the head just as easily as he can snake an arm around an exposed neck to choke him; there is no question he's of the "genuine future" variety. A clean-cut, underground veteran and star in the making.

For fans of this new but exceedingly popular sport, there's a smorgasbord of offerings broadcast on SpikeTV, Showtime, and various other cable networks every month, and sometimes there's even a helping of it on CBS primetime. But take the grittiest of those selections and it's all still so sanitized compared to what Peter's been producing, the fruits of his illicit labor succulent and compelling and subversive like that apple Eve shared with Adam. "My league prepares people for mixed martial arts," he says. "My league prepares people how to fight for real," and there's that word again. It's unsanctioned and underground, and like a fist to the mouth that drops you to your knees and prompts you to spit teeth onto the canvas, it's most certainly real. But for all the UCL has done in giving aspirants a taste of what battle is like, a fighter can only go so far beating up fellow undergrounders. To move up, to paying gigs and shiny championship belts and stays at the Tropicana in Atlantic City, and maybe even further up the food chain to the holiest of holies, the Mount Olympus where the gods of mixed martial arts sit—the UFC—one ultimately has to move on. One has to fight where it's sanctioned, and face those bigger fish in that bigger pond.

Thanks to New York City's underground fight circuit, I know James can fight for real. But the time has come for him to take his mouthpiece and gloves and fight shorts and compete elsewhere, where there are rules and you don't have to worry about the police breaking things up. Has his tenure in the Underground Combat League made him ready?

A TALE OF TWO FIGHT SHOWS

Two shows in two days, a highly regulated amateur event on Saturday night in a drafty convention hall in Northern New Jersey, and a UCL at a martial arts gym in the Bronx on Sunday night, so unregulated and Wild West that there was no ring, just a mat with forty or so spectators gathered around, and when the fights got underway the gym owner pulled down the front gate and locked us all in. Two shows on opposite ends of the spectrum.

I don't know why I cared so much, why I was worried and concerned and bothered that Kirkland had suffered an injury to his eye and that it was now almost swollen shut, red when he forced it open with sweaty fingers. Kirkland was a nice enough guy, distant and brusque when in his pre-fight zone and approachable afterward, when he was usually the victor courtesy of his wrestling ability and relentless ground and pound. But he was quiet, shy like an introvert or outcast or someone not quite sure about this violence he visited upon people, and when he fought he rarely had anyone cheering for him other than those who just liked blood. I don't know anything about him other than that he sometimes trained at the Tiger Schulmann's school in Manhattan, wore black and red "TSK" shorts but did not represent their fight team.

"Kirkland, you have to get that eye looked at," I told him. He looked at me with his good one, nodded. Three rounds of getting kicked, punched, elbowed, choked, and twisted had left him breathless and battered, his black skin glistening and the veins in his thick arms bulging. "Where do you live?" I asked.

"Here in the Bronx," he muttered, offering up no more than that, and I was worried that he wouldn't go to the emergency room, concerned that he could have serious damage, bothered that he was there alone and that no one would look after him. This edition of unsanctioned combat had featured one grappling-only match and three limited-rules bouts of varying degrees of skill level, and Kirkland's bout had been the final one, the *pièce de resistance* that saw him fight to a draw against Joe Funaro. The show, though, was over, and it was time for me to pack up my pad and pencil and head to the subway. But . . . I was hesitant, my reluctance sprouting from the tiny streaks of red in the white of Kirkland's eye.

In 2000, a forward-thinking New Jersey commission honcho named Larry Hazzard Sr. and his consigliere Nick Lembo ironed out rules for professional MMA matches—the Unified Rules of Mixed Martial Arts used by the UFC and most major promotions today—and in 2006 they repeated that progressive feat with an amateur version of mixed martial arts. A league for pugilistic newcomers flourished almost overnight. Sure, purists may have decried the wealth of restrictions, like no kicking to the head while standing or no punching to the head when a fighter is down (rendering ground and pound null and void), but if you looked past those safeguards, and the required shin pads and short three-minute rounds, you had something far more appetizing to both the cautious noob and ill-prepared martial fool alike.

Fast-forward to Saturday night, the day before the UCL and Kirkland's injury. Of all the promoters who had tried their best to put out a consistent product and establish a brand, Carl's had risen to the top, and tonight his December 13th Asylum Fight League show would feature a mishmash of twenty-four fighters and all the cheering friends and family one could ever tolerate. I wandered around, an hour before the first scheduled bout, the calm before the storm, really the best time to see the gears in motion.

The convention hall was cavernous, meant for multi-stalled flea markets or some other equally massive endeavor, and rows and rows of metal folding chairs encircled the cage like worshippers around the likeness of an ancient deity. Backstage, the fighters were gathered in a carpeted and plain ballroom short on tables and chairs, listening while the head referee, a karate old-schooler named Donnie, went over the rules. Most already had their hands wrapped. Most already had that look, that demeanor of anxiety and maybe fear. Soon they would be out there getting punched in the face, risking a knockout or other loss of dignity and pride, and now, before riding into battle, was when they mustered their courage and steeled themselves for the worst. Pre-fight and you can't expect too much from a fighter other than a handshake or a nod, but Katz, the coach from Queens, greeted me. Carmine, a jiu-jitsu instructor, greeted me. Eddy, a coach from Lodi, New Jersey, greeted me. Lembo popped into the ballroom, the final incarnation of the fight card on a printout in his hand, and he quickly disappeared, while the Tiger Schulmann contingent had staked out another room as their own to warm up their fighters and congregate. Back in the main hall a few hundred spectators had filled the metal folding chairs.

Cageside, two doctors, employees of the New Jersey State Athletic Control Board and experienced with combative sports injuries like inner-city trauma surgeons are experienced with gunshot wounds, talked. To compete here, tonight, you had to register with a sanctioning organization called the United States Kickboxing Association (to which the New Jersey athletic commission had farmed out most of the responsibility and liability; that all would change in the coming year with the passing of USKBA founder Paul Rosner. After that, it was a total NJSACB-run operation). To compete tonight, you needed paperwork including approval from your trainer, stating that you were ready, and approval from your physician, stating that you wouldn't keel over and die the second your heart rate elevated. To compete tonight you needed all that, and in return you got a cage, a ramp for your grand entrance, a DJ to play the song of your choice, a medical professional to look you over before and after, a trained referee, and even an ambulance waiting in the wings to cart your crippled body away if the need arose. And aside from all the bells and whistles and frills, you got an unpaid amateur fight, much safer than a paid pro fight and a world away from a *vale tudo* match. What more could you want?

I got the text from Peter a few days before his Sunday show, more clandestine than usual (if that was possible) and with instructions to not tell a soul. The location was new, small, under the radar like a stop on Harriet Tubman's railroad would be under the radar. A few weeks prior, at a legislative roundtable for the legalization of MMA in New York State, the first

words out of New York State Athletic Commission Chairwoman
Melvina Lathan's mouth were a lament at the abundance of
underground shows in the state, and that plus a letter on athletic commission stationery to nearly every boxing gym
owner proclaiming the unlawfulness of MMA bouts had
forced Peter to ratchet up the secrecy. I couldn't tell if that
made the UCL more of a forbidden fruit, savored by those
lucky enough to get a bite, but it certainly made it exclusive.

To compete in the UCL you just had to show up. You got
no bells, no whistles or frills, and this time around you didn't
even get a ring, which was just fine to those few on the inside
of the martial arts school at the northernmost edge of the
Bronx. When I arrived with ace photog Anil, Peter gave us a
tour, informing us that, yes, everyone would have to take off
their shoes so as not to ruin the school's wall-to-wall mats,
and yes, audience members would have to line up against the
mirrored wall to act as a buffer lest fighters tumble into the
glass. In a tiny locker room in back, Kirkland sat on the floor,
headphones on and eyes distant, and we exchanged nods as I
was led downstairs, to the unfinished basement where the
fighters would warm up (by this point Peter had honed his
flair for the dramatic, and nothing says "underground show"
more than combatants skipping rope and hitting pads amidst
torn up concrete and debris and shadows). Upstairs, Kevin
arrived, as did the Funaro brothers and a Tae Kwon Do stylist named Arjang. When I asked Arjang who he trained under,
he mentioned Ray Longo, a high-level MMA and kickboxing
coach from Long Island who taught UFC welterweight champ
Matt Serra how to strike.

Undefeated UCL fighter Josh strolled in (roll footage of
Josh bloodying his opponent, saying immediately after his
bout how much of a thrill it was to smash someone). I won-

dered aloud to Josh if he was allowed to be here, as his day job had been none too pleased at his extracurricular activities, and he told me his day job—like Fox 5 News—could kiss his ass. "They caught me right after I fought so of course I was hyped up, but they cut out the part where I said I train every day for this." Josh wasn't here to compete, he was just there to watch, but he would end up cornering Kirkland when the time came.

Peter handed a stopwatch to a Brooklynite with a shaved head, a friendly white kid named Adam who looked rough but was very likeable, deputizing him as the official time-keeper. Adam had fought and lost three times in the UCL, and because of an injured knee, injured courtesy of an NYPD officer's baton, he was relegated to the sidelines this time around. Jerry jotted down the identities of the competitors and match-ups were made. The two most skilled were Kirkland and Joe, so they would be the main event. The other bouts fell into place like pieces of an oversimplified puzzle.

As if on cue, down came the front gate. Peter addressed the small number in attendance, the invite-only crowd, mostly men but a few young women, too, each one of them somehow connected to one of the fighters. Then, with everyone in their socks, gathered around the edges of the mat or lined up against the mirrors, cell phone cameras at the ready and cheers and respectfulness on the tips of their tongues, it was on, and Jerry shouted for the first two on the list to step up and fight.

A young Hispanic named Alejandro, whip-thin and muscular like a greyhound, crouched low and repeatedly shot in, taking his heavier opponent to the mat again and again until he snagged an armbar. Next up was Kevin, who, at 210 pounds, engaged in a sloppy free-for-all against a 260-pounder, the two stumbling around and falling at my feet. Before three minutes had expired, Kevin had his arm snaked under the bigger man's chin, forcing a tap out with a choke as I looked down at them. They rose, embraced, and the vanquished raised the victor's hand acknowledging defeat. Everyone cheered, as much for the mutual respect as for the action. Arjang stepped up, squared off against a shorter man in a karate uniform and a black belt. Before the event, the shorter man professed to represent some obscure style, its name possibly something Korean. (Months later I would run into him at the school of a prominent jiu-jitsu fighter, but his silence would clue me in about not mentioning his UCL participation.) Arjang and the shorter man traded timid kicks and occasional punches, neither looking to brawl or commit to anything that could leave them exposed, and all the while one of Arjang's corner men was narrating into his phone. In between rounds, he put the phone to the out-of-breath fighter's ear. Chuckles and laughs from some of us watching because what the hell could be so important that Arjang had to take a call between rounds? At the end of the third round Arjang was awarded the decision. It was time for Kirkland and Joe.

Back in New Jersey and Katz's fighter, a UCL veteran, was waging war against a Tiger Schulmann's MMA instructor from Long Island. The Tiger Schulmannn representative was a superior striker and stalked his prey around the cage, delivering blows like a predator picking apart its future dinner, but Katz's fighter was aces in the wrestling department and when not backing up and eating leather, he swooped in to dump the instructor onto the canvas. In between rounds, the fast-talking Katz administered Vaseline to the ridges and fresh abrasions adorning his ward's face, the kid inhaling deeply, exhaling, trying his best to catch his breath.

Then it was the affable Eddy kneeling there before his own fighter on the stool, Eddy articulating instructions on how best to not get blasted in the jaw while going for take-downs.

Then it was the easygoing Carmine and his student, a near-flawless grappler, Carmine directing him to keep up the pressure and reinforcing to him that his opponent sitting on the stool in the opposite corner was getting the worst of it. Years ago, when MMA was new in the Garden State, Katz and Carmine were the trainers behind a warrior named Kaream Ellington, whose climb up a very short mountain was stalled when Kaream met Eddy in the cage and lost via submission, and now time had made them all the older, wiser relatives in a family, an incestuous pool of coaches and competitors, where chances are the person standing across from you was someone you had already fought or someone you had trained under or someone who fought your trainer, or whatever, ad infinitum. Stay in the game long enough and you would encounter everyone in nearly every possible role, training partner or coach, enemy or ally.

Within the cage, a tiny green-haired Tiger Schulmann representative named Louis Gaudinot engaged in the kind of battle you'd expect to see if Speedy Gonzales ever fought the Tazmanian Devil. Gaudinot and his opponent tossed each other around and fired off frenzied strikes until Gaudinot executed a graceful, picture-perfect, and deadly accurate spinning backfist (so graceful a ballerina would've wept at the sight of it), and his opponent ate it to the side of his head and dropped like a sack of potatoes, out freakin' cold. The exclamation point of an ending was still hanging there in the air when everyone and their mother went bananas in the audience behind me. The doctors were at the fallen combatant's side almost instantly. Even Gaudinot got a look-over, maybe to see if he had damaged his forearm nearly decapitating his opponent, and the knocked-out fighter was moved to a stool where he regained his senses and stood, and he and Gaudinot sought each other out for an exchange of respect and appreciation.

It was a much kinder, gentler, and safer beast now, but it wasn't always so. When Eddy fought Kaream back in 2001, it was for a sanctioned event in Atlantic City, an event thick with commission oversight and responsibility. Yet shows like that were rare then. Most of Eddy's bouts, and Kaream's and Carmine's, were of the unsanctioned variety (Eddy could boast of over seventy fights to his name, the majority outside the purview of the NJSACB), and back in that earlier era a knockout or other serious injury wasn't something that would lead to any sort of suspension. If the perpetually grinning Eddy got clobbered at a BAMA Fight Night, the only thing keeping him from getting into the ring the next day would be his concerned wife. Tonight, though, it was a different story entirely. Despite coming away victorious, Katz's kid was told by the commission doctors that he must get an echocardiogram before he could fight again, and Gaudinot's victim was suspended for thirty days and ordered to get a neurological exam. As of December of 2008, there had been only one death worldwide in a sanctioned mixed martial arts bout (Sam Vasquez, who died from injuries sustained in a fight in Texas), and with the lengths of medical screening a fighter must undergo, both before and after he stepped into the ring or cage and threw down, it was not hard to see why the sport had generated far fewer deaths than boxing or football or even cheerleading.

The Bronx. Full-time Stony Brook University student and history major Joe had a ways to go before he could catch up to his brother, James, in terms of ring time, but he was putting in the effort. "I want to get paid for it one day and make a lot of money," he would say to me afterward. "But even if I don't, I do it because it's fun. I love the competition of it."

Competition was what Kirkland gave him, and then some. Again and again Kirkland ducked low, shot, wrapped his arms around Joe's legs, and pulled him to the mat to pound him, a strange sort of a dance with the white kid from Long Island playing the role of "man delivering vicious elbows and punches from the bottom." As the combatants moved from one area to another the crowd followed, a living organism enthralled and cheering its warring nucleus in three-minute increments, and pausing and letting the nucleus breathe during that one-minute rest between rounds. At one point James, no more than a foot away from his brother, saw Joe waver, perhaps a flicker of fatigue or exasperation on his twin's face, and he started screaming, "There is no God but you, Joseph! No God but you!" The emotion behind the words hinted of anger like the Pope hinted at Christianity, and while I knew that honor, integrity, and sportsmanship prevented James from standing up and kicking Kirkland off his brother like a soccer ball, there was really nothing stopping James from booting his sibling in the teeth if Joe were to tap out.

The fighters scrambled to their feet and threw strikes, and Joe accidentally poked Kirkland in the eye with an errant thumb. Kirkland recoiled, covered his eye with a gloved hand, and Joe backed off, his palms out in the universal sign of "Whoa, sorry." Jerry stepped in to make the separation official, and after Kirkland was given time to recover, the fight resumed. Time soon ran out. The two were battered and scraped and out of breath, and Jerry consulted with a couple of random people around the mat—the judges, as it were. He returned, pulled Kirkland and the Funaro brother to him by their wrists, and raised both arms in the air. The fight was declared a draw.

No one argued the decision. This one was close. Joe and Kirkland hugged and thanked each other, sincere in their appreciation of the performance the other had forced them to give. When the great Jigoro Kano created judo in the late 1800s, one of the tenets he had put forth was the concept of "mutual welfare and benefit," the idea that dispensing some butt-kicking to each other would ultimately make everyone better at kicking butt, and if Kano were alive today, in the Bronx at this secluded gym hosting an underground fight, he'd have recognized that hug for what it was. And once he got over the fact that he had been dead for the last seventy years, he probably would've smiled.

11

"We're building a real strong following, and what makes us unique—regardless of it being in New Jersey—is the fact that it's a league for a fighter, by a fighter," said Carl, the maestro of amateur MMA in the Garden State. I had called him at home after meeting a few times in person, curious about his perspective. "I grew up in fighting and fought my entire life," he said. He went on to reveal that he was a former boxer and kickboxer who went from owning martial arts schools to operating Asylum full-time, and it was clear from talking with him that his amateur league was far more akin to a passion than to work.

"I actually started off with a different company," said the thirty-six-year-old promoter. "It was New Breed Fighters. We had our first event, I had [early UFC veteran] Guy Mezger at the event, it was in Vorhees, New Jersey, and it went extremely well. I grew one company, which was New Breed Fighters, into a really popular circuit in New Jersey. I kind of had a falling-out with the partner I had on board, and out of the ashes of something dying out came Asylum Fight League, which has been amazing. We're going to celebrate our first-year anniversary in April and we're at thirteen shows now. We just got our Pennsylvania license. The company has just exploded because there are good people in there and every-body's got a good heart toward what our entire mission is. Our mission is to take an amateur fighter, cultivate them, bring them up, get them as much experience as possible, and get them an opportunity to go pro."

I asked him to condense the secret of Asylum's success down into a few sentences. He paused, probably considering his answer, then fired back with: "As comfortable as you are walking into a living room, you're that comfortable walking into our arenas. It feels like home. The fighters are comfort-able there, and they're just so passionate. They're as passion-ate as I am about having the show. When they fight, I fight. When they win, I win."

Throughout our conversation, his enthusiasm never wavered, and I asked for Carl's thoughts on the restrictive rules amateurs in New Jersey must abide by. "Nick Lembo and Paul Rosner [of the United States Kickboxing Association] came up with the rules for New Jersey, and I totally give them the utmost respect and recognition. Without them, we really wouldn't be established as well. I agree that there shouldn't be ground and pound in the amateurs just because of the trauma to the brain, and if you turn around and look at it, eliminating ground and pound in the amateurs helps a fighter hone their skills on the ground without having too much consequence." He added: "There's a lot of good pros out there now who honed their skills in the amateurs. They made their skills while the consequences weren't as high as in the pros, so they were able to adjust their games and build up their games and find their weaknesses so they don't have the same weaknesses as pros."

I asked Carl about the brass ring, the ultimate goal for him and his sanctioned organization. On that, he didn't hesitate. "I want to have a true national championship held in Las Vegas where we can turn around and do like a draft, and invite Dana White and all the promoters of the big pro leagues, and have an MMA draft where all the amateurs—whoever wins— they get an opportunity to get a bigger contract than if they just walked off the street being a no-name. Just like in a football draft, where they say, 'Congratulations, you've just been signed to the Redskins,' well, I want to say, 'Congratulations, you've just been signed to the UFC.' I want people to come in from every state and say, 'I want to fight in Asylum before I go pro. That's the true proving grounds for me to go to before I become a professional.'"

"I really, really love to fight," James told me days after his brother's UCL bout, and he went on to describe the path that led him into mixed martial arts competition. At twenty-two he had gone from high school wrestling to karate to Brazilian Jiu-Jitsu, and unlike his college-student brother, James lived and breathed combat sports full-time in the form of training and teaching it. "When I started doing Brazilian Jiu-Jitsu I wanted to compete in something," said the Long Islander. "I missed competing like when I wrestled, and I wanted to test myself. I just wanted a different outlet for martial arts. So I went to a Brazilian Jiu-Jitsu tournament in New Jersey. I got two matches. After about six months of training, I won my first match and lost my second match and then I went home. I drove all the way to New Jersey and drove all the way back and spent like twelve hours there the whole day, and I said, 'Wow, this really sucks. I just spent twelve hours and all I got was maybe four minutes of mat time.' So I decided that if I did a mixed martial arts match, I could still do my Brazilian Jiu-Jitsu inside the mixed martial arts match, but I wouldn't have to wait twelve hours to do it."

The brothers had cast their hats into the MMA ring at amateur events in New Jersey, Ohio, and Upstate New York before turning to the limited-rules *vale tudo* realm of the Underground Combat League. "I think most amateur organizations shouldn't do *vale tudo*," said James. "I think *vale tudo* is something separate that, when you feel you're ready for it or it's something you want to do, that's your own personal decision. But on a whole, for the sport, I think amateur rules are kind of crazy. In New Jersey, you shouldn't have to wear shin pads if you're not allowed to kick to the head. I don't like that you can't ground and pound to the head. I'm okay with the fact that there's no elbows or knees allowed—I think that's perfect for amateurs. I guess I really don't care too much because I got the UCL around the corner." I asked him why he liked the Underground Combat League. As fight shows go, this one was far more dangerous than most, and for the risk involved, getting paid zilch almost defied reason. "One, because it's right here," he said. "And two, because it's awesome. It's pretty much just super-awesome-deluxe to fight in the UCL because it's everything. You can do whatever you want. It's really the ultimate test of fighting."

"I like that there's really nobody there," said Joe. "It's not as much of a show. At the last one there was no ring, it was just a mat. This one there wasn't even entrance music, you just stepped onto the mat and fought. How often do you get to say you did that?"

I recalled James's rant while his brother fought and the emotion there, and I asked him about it. "I was going to kick his ass," he said, adding a chuckle almost as an afterthought. "I love it when he fights. I think it's awesome when he fights. We really got animated during this fight because this was Joe's first fight using elbows and knees and everything. This was only his third fight. I fought Kirkland and it was my ninth fight, and I'm sure Kirkland's had five or six fights at least. So this was only Joe's third fight, he was nervous, this was the first time fighting under these rules. And he even admitted afterward that there were a couple points where he'd wanted to give up because he'd never been through the first round anyway. It was really tough for him and I could see that he was kind of teetering on the brink of wanting to give up, so I was telling him that I really didn't care if he won or lost, but if he didn't try and go out there and fight, then we were going to beat him up. I don't care too much about the winning or losing as long as you fight."

"It's intimidating sometimes," Joe countered. "It's a little showmanship, but it's honestly how I talk with him and my friends.

"You could see it in his eyes that he wanted to give up for like a split second, and then he bounced right back—which is awesome. He learned a lot from that match, I'm sure, about what he could do."

To his credit, one thing Joe could not do was take advantage of his inadvertent eye gouge of Kirkland. "I felt it right away and saw him back up," Joe said. "I knew instantly I hit him with my thumb. That would be pretty fucked up to do to go after him. It's not a street fight. Even though it's the underground and it has limited rules, you're not out to maim."

Though only the Hudson River separates New York from New Jersey, an amateur MMA show in one was a world away from an amateur show in the other, with the disparity in medical care the greatest gulf. Suffer an injury at an Asylum Fight League outing and physicians were all over you; suffer an injury at a UCL and you were on your own. I asked the brothers if that bothered them, if it factored into their decision to compete at Peter's show at all.

"I have health insurance so I know that I'm pretty much covered with whatever happens to me," said Joe. "But if you don't have health insurance, then why are you fighting?"

"I don't care because I pay for my own health insurance, and I have really good health insurance for that reason," said James. "I make sure I get my blood tests done, just for myself to make sure I'm okay. The thing with fighting unsanctioned is, yes, there's a risk of getting hurt, but I don't really hold it against the UCL if I get hurt because I know going into it there's no false pretenses. No one's saying I have to get health insurance, no one's saying anything. I'm twenty-two and I'm old enough to make those decisions. If someone goes in there knowing they could get hurt, and they don't have insurance and they get hurt, they're out of luck. It's their own fault. I think you should have all the information before you go into that fight—which I think everybody does. They know what they're doing. Let them do it."

III

Not long after, upon hearing that one of his students had competed in the UCL, Coach Longo issued a statement blasting underground shows. He also banished that fighter from his school. Ring of Combat promoter Lou Neglia followed up with a press release of his own, a one-two punch combo aimed at those hoping to use unsanctioned fight shows as a stepping-stone to bigger (and paying) gigs.

To Whom It May Concern:

I have the best wishes in mind for the entire mixed martial arts community for the New Year.

I have great hopes for the continued growth of the sport in my home state of New York and nationwide.

With that in mind, I must announce that I will no longer permit contestants to compete in my event (Ring of Combat) if they still choose to compete in unregulated, unsanctioned, or illegal events. For example, if a contestant chooses to compete in a UCL event, they will no longer be welcome to compete on future events that I promote.

There is no valid reason for a contestant to compete in an unsafe and unregulated atmosphere. Those who choose to do so are not acting in the best interests of the future growth and acceptance of this sport.

   This policy will go into effect as of the date of this writing.

> Sincerely,
> Louis Neglia
> Promoter, Ring of Combat

In the year prior, Lembo had put out word that anyone competing in unsanctioned events would not be allowed to compete as an amateur in New Jersey without at least shelling out the bucks for the expensive medicals a pro fighter must have (upwards of 500 bucks more in medical costs). This, plus Longo and Lou's statements, left no room for doubt as to where the long-running UCL stood in the minds of the "big boys" of the sport.

A paramedic present for the event had looked Kirkland's eye over ("Um, yeah, it's messed up."), but it was not enough, and I didn't leave the gym in the Bronx on that Sunday night until Jerry reassured me that he would personally take Kirkland to the emergency room. Nearly everyone else had filtered out, and the few stragglers left behind were shaking hands with Peter and voicing praise or gratitude. There was nowhere else to see live *vale tudo* bouts within New York City limits, and only those who really wanted to be here ended up here—definite grounds for the kind words and thanks. "I will take him," said Jerry. "I promise." So after shaking Kirkland's hand one last time, I departed. His eye was completely swollen shut, and I feared he would need stitches or surgery on one of the most sensitive and vulnerable parts of the human body, yet at least I knew he was going to get some form of medical attention.

Peter's text came later that night.

FYI: Kirkland had a popped blood vessel. No stitching required.

TSK

Tiger Schulmann's Mixed Martial Arts was formerly Tiger Schulmann's Karate (TSK for short). No self-respecting member would dare compete in the underground, they're too legit and above the board. But to know Mike Fischetti, James's opponent at that upcoming sanctioned show in New Jersey, to know what's in store for James when the cage door shuts, you need to know where Mike came from. You need to know TSK.

Fans will shell out the cash for a ticket to see Tito Ortiz or Ken Shamrock or Forrest Griffin or Randy Couture based on star power alone, but for the ROCs and UCLs of the world it's all about the fighters' families, friends, and often students reaching into their pockets. Promotions live and die before solving this riddle, their death a dark comedy as matchmakers bounce blindly, ignorantly and unwittingly along the learning curve before their money runs out. The smarter ones will sit in the audience at rival events, gauging fan response to the fighters and tracking those big ticket sellers down to make them offers. Follow the path traversed by nearly every dollar in a promoter's bank account and the trail will lead you back to a consumer with a stake in the fight, someone eager to see his buddy, his cousin, his dear sensei scrap. It really is no mystery. The truth is, a Gracie teaching at Renzo's academy has a wealth of students eager to see him strut his stuff, and even those without disciples, like competitors Doug and Tom, will draw a decent number of nearest and dearest to the trough. It's business, simple economics, a double-edged sword of product and demand that disembowels with more frequency than it rewards.

But without fail, a promoter has struck gold if he's got a Tiger Schulmann fighter on his card. As fight teams go, they're the brass ring capable of saving a show, the number of empty seats versus butts turning into the kind of math that makes a promoter grin and light up a cigar. And forget it if the Tiger Schulmann fighter on the card is Lyman Good.

There are harsh lessons to be learned in the ring or the cage, and if you happened to be standing across from Lyman, he was always the one conducting the lesson. His skills were diverse, his conditioning unparalleled, and his drive an unstoppable force. At Lyman's debut at Ring of Combat 9 back in 2005, the three-round drubbing he delivered prompted his opponent to puke in the middle of the fight, an abrupt cascade of slime right there on the canvas. At Ring of Combat 10, the force of his knockout right cross sent his opponent sailing through the ropes in the second round. He won that one with a fractured hand—fractured from his very first punch in the opening round—and his cold, angry eyes seemed to reflect battles far tougher already fought and won within. Of the 40,000-plus Tiger Schulmann students, the chiseled Lyman had risen to the top, and his mere presence on a fight card implied legions of rabid fans shouting "TSK! TSK!"

"It's not just a fighter going out there, it's an army," Lyman said, stating the obvious. We were sitting in an office at a Tiger Schulmann school in Greenwich Village, the flagship TSK outpost where he taught, and I had caught him at the tail end of one of his usual long days. Outside, students practiced maneuvers involving submission escapes and punch avoidance in one of the big, matted rooms, and kids and parents gathered in the waiting area to boast and laugh. Now three years removed from his first fight and Lyman could open up to reporters without subjecting them to a shiver-inducing stare. He had gotten to the point where he could speak freely and, if the situation warranted it, laugh. "There's a lot of students, people who you've supported and who you've taught all the time, and you go out there and fight and do what it is that you preach to them. When you fight, you're not just fighting for yourself. You're fighting for the people you've taught."

Throngs of students notwithstanding, Lyman did it for a bit more. If there's an archetype of what makes a fighter, a template coded into genes, or a set pattern of experiences that draws a person into a life of hard training and even harder fights, then this twenty-four-year-old from the 'hood of Spanish Harlem was the model mixed martial artist, a model made more complete by whatever emotional turmoil an absentee father, a few years of military school, and the need to support his mother and sisters had generated to fuel his fire. And you needed all that fuel to keep you going when your days revolved around four hours of sparring, grappling, and nonstop calisthenics followed by six hours of teaching. You needed that fuel, otherwise you crumbled.

Almost a year later I ran into Lyman at an Asylum Fight League event in Northern New Jersey. Around was us a nightclub, with a cage set up in the middle of what would

normally be a dance floor full of Jersey caricatures of cool.
The music blared between fights and the crowd, pressed up
against the cage, sipped beer from bottles and downed shots
of God knows what. I leaned in and asked Lyman how his
training was going. He had been on ice for the past year, signing
on the dotted line for a contract with EliteXC only to have Elite-
XC go the way of the dinosaur, but some new Latino-centric
promotion called the Bellator Fighting Championships had
scooped him up to star in a 170-pound eight-man tournament
to be broadcast on ESPN's Deportes channel. Lyman smirked.
His jaw was square, stubbled, and carved out of wood, and
his black T-shirt bore the familiar emblem of a roaring tiger
and "Tiger Schulmann's Mixed Martial Arts" in red and white
lettering on his chest. "I've been sleeping in a cage," he said.
"Shihan thought it would be a good idea to get me focused."

Shihan, a.k.a. Danny "Tiger" Schulmann. The head of one
of the biggest, most successful martial arts school chains in
the country, a man revered within the organization and
respected without for turning a background in Kyokushin
Karate into an empire of logos, chanting students, and pristine
training centers. To someone on the outside it might all seem
cult-like. To those seeking entrance through one of their forty-
eight schools throughout New York, New Jersey, Pennsylvania, Connecticut, and Florida, it's a gauntlet of hard sell and
rules and structure. To a sports writer, watching their end
product throwing leather and orchestrating submissions and
finagling escapes in the heat of battle, it's the evolution of
commercialized combat into absolute effectiveness. Say what
you want about Schulmann—and people do—but he's stayed
ahead of the curve, thrusting students into kickboxing and
boxing bouts to hone their skills when they were karate, and

thrusting them into kickboxing, boxing, and grappling competitions when MMA popped up.

In a realm where martial arts lineage can speak volumes, and in an era when who taught you how to grapple can bear more weight than what you can actually do on the mat, the big question mark hanging over TSK is where their knowledge of submissions came from. Initially, it was trips to Las Vegas, where Danny and his brother Ronnie absorbed techniques from jiu-jitsu black belt John Lewis (the World Fighting Alliance promoter), techniques they regurgitated and drilled back east. But as time went by, their fight team attracted all manner of studs, like Rick Dellagatta, a two-time member of the Olympic wrestling team, and assorted submission specialists were sucked into their orbit. Soon their system had its own viable no-gi style. The running joke back in the nineties was the concept of the "McDojo," a money-making scheme disguised as a martial arts school teaching "real fighting." The gag included overweight instructors, counseling on which karate chop and kata worked best against multiple attackers. The gag included children declared "deadly weapons" by virtue of their belt status. The gag included worthless training, and would-be fighters got creamed when reality took them down to the ground and beat the ever-loving crap out of them. In the Northeast, when MMA was new, most labeled Tiger Schulmann's Karate a McDojo—and if one looked only at their commercialized product and utterly devoted students, they fit the bill. But they can fight and they can win in the confines of an MMA bout, and that alone defies the very essence of the word.

In October of 2002 I witnessed firsthand Team Tiger Schulmann's true power, which manifested itself at a grappling-only tournament called Grapplers Quest. A byproduct of Brazilian Jiu-Jitsu's rise in popularity, Grapplers Quest pits one grappler against another—wrestlers, judo, and sambo players, jiu-jitsu specialists—and if no submission is secured within the time limit, points are tallied based on positions gained. In a high school gymnasium in Bayonne there were six different mats simultaneously active with nearly 600 competitors, upwards of 1,100 spectators watching from matside or sitting in the bleachers, and prohibitions against striking and slamming. And when one of Schulmann's students was disqualified by a referee for an infraction (a slam), a heated argument ensued with event promoter Brian Cimins siding unequivocally with his official. From my vantage point on the next mat over I heard clear as day the anger in Schulmann's voice, a booming declaration of "We are done!" Picture a few hundred participants in TSK gear—black and white Lycra shorts, rashguards, T-shirts emblazoned with the face of a snarling tiger—picture all of them, roughly a third of the gymnasium's inhabitants, stopping whatever they're doing and filing out. One, in the midst of a match and working for a submission from below his opponent, even apologized, a sincere "I'm sorry" as he stood up and joined his departing team (the referee declared the other guy the winner by default). Picture that, and think about how, thanks to one questionable referee call that Schulmann refused to let slide, Cimins would never have another Schulmann presence at his tournaments again. As spectators pay to watch and competitors pay to compete, that's one healthy chunk of change no longer going into Cimins's pocket. That's not just power; that's Thulsa Doom-commanding-a-follower-to-jump-off-a-cliff-and-ordering-Conan-crucified-on-the-Tree-of-Woe power.

(Days later I made my way out to TSK headquarters, a

martial arts gym/office hybrid in a New Jersey industrial park to get Schulmann's side of the story. After sitting in on a black belt instructor class involving a wide range of striking and grappling techniques, I was led to another room and shown a shaky home video of the match at the center of the controversy. Schulmann pointed out that when the infraction allegedly occurred, the referee was looking away, and the TSK student was disqualified solely on the opposing coach's word that a foul had been committed. That was the crux of his grievance.)

When someone steps into the ring or cage or onto the mat wearing the Tiger Schulmann insignia, he's part of a family, a loud, and at times intimidating, family. There is, of course, the child and soccer mom component, the giant-sized demographic that happily gobbles up the discipline and fitness aspect of the product along with the packaging. They're the meat and potatoes of the organization. They pay the bills, as the comparatively small number of fighting students alone would barely generate enough revenue to keep the lights on in one academy. But it works. The business model is solid, like a 143-pound Golden Gloves finalist boxer's abs are solid, and whether you walk into one of their gyms and are turned off by the sales pitch or you devour it voraciously, you can't help but marvel at the machine. Schulmann, alongside his brother Ron and everyone else who's had a hand in the business, has made it all work.

Grapplers Quest was my first exposure to their power, but my first up-close look at Team Tiger Schulmann in action was at a Reality Fighting event in 2002, years before Lyman's era, in an airy convention center in Wildwood, New Jersey. Outside, the chilly November night breeze off the ocean, on the edge of a town that barely exists when it's not summer.

Within, the raucous sounds of the first female MMA bout ever in the Garden State. Within, TSK's Laura D'Auguste stepped into the ring to face a Renzo Gracie–trained girl. Laura was older and blond, focused like someone with a job to do, while Jiu-Jitsu Girl was young and dark-haired and maybe a little more nervous-looking. The audience was packed with supporters in black T-shirts sporting yellow TSK lettering, shouting "TSK! TSK!" in unison, a stark comparison to Jiu-Jitsu Girl's cheering section, which bordered on the nonexistent. When not training at her Long Island outpost, Laura was a nurse and the single mother to a teenage daughter. Jiu-Jitsu Girl made money with private wrestling sessions, roughing up clients for an hourly rate.

The month prior was the mass walkout from Grapplers Quest and my subsequent visit to their headquarters. Now, however, was when I saw them throw down. One can lie all they want in the dojo, brag relentlessly and boast and promise and predict, but what happens in the ring is truth—the ring never lies—and in 2002 lies were still being peeled away like dead skin on a piece of sweet, luscious, adrenaline-filled fruit. Pre-Ultimate Fighter, a year into Dana White's reign as the UFC's king, and the kinks were still being worked out as to what worked and what didn't, what was viable and what wasn't, and though the Brazilian Jiu-Jitsu moniker was still like royalty, akin to saying you're a Kennedy or a Rockefeller, things like shootfighting, Muay Thai, sambo, and Greco-Roman were bandied about like they, too, could hold the answers. Come to a fight show and you'd see them all. There were the disciples of Bart Vale, a big American who learned his moves in the Japanese pro-wrestling circuit (where pro-wrestling is rougher and more real like a ladies' night dance floor grind in a Bedford-Stuyvesant nightclub is rougher and

more real). There were the brawlers, infused with confidence
because their evenings spent putting down drunks and
quaffing beers in Jersey Shore bars had left them confident and
with reputations as hard-asses; the wrestlers, champions in
high school or members of some college team, well-conditioned
and full of themselves because they could survive whatever
hell their coaches devised; the judo grapplers, used to fighting
while wearing a gi and incapable of pulling off most of their
moves once competition entered the realm of the shirtless; the
kickboxers, praying to God they'd never get taken down; and
of course the karate refugees, some of them earnest, some of
them delusional as to what would work and sad casualties in
the war on the esoteric.

So far on this November night a stocky Hispanic Tiger
Schulmann fighter named Elvis had pounded out a win
against a fighter from Philadelphia after five minutes of brutality. So far, rough-and-tumble TSK scrapper Dave had fallen
prey to a Hail Mary leglock in two minutes, and in the final
bout of the evening the team would earn its first MMA championship belt via a fight-ending cut, a cut sustained when
Zach used razor-sharp striking to land a kick to a wrestler's
face. But right now the Earth was rotating around Laura and
her eight-minute battering of Jiu-Jitsu Girl, all the perfectly
timed sprawls used to counter every takedown, the constant
stream of punches chipping away at the jiu-jitsu femme's
veneer, the tenacity, the crowd rendered completely and
utterly insane. Laura would become Team Tiger Schulmann's
first superstar, a warrior prototype and the original, purest
example of the organization's ability to assemble well-
rounded mixed martial artists where none existed before.

For a generation weaned on commercialized martial arts,
MMA was a big, fat reality sandwich, a sandwich that more

often than not made Tae Kwon Do faux-badasses and kung
fu fakes gag and choke. Yet for an organization with thousands of members, and the resources to mold the cream of
their in-house crop into warriors, dining heartily on that sandwich was inevitable, each progressive bite savored. That first
night seeing them in action in Wildwood, it wasn't hard to
see what they'd eventually become. The rise of this new sport
meant the old paradigms of combat were shifting, changing,
and no longer would you be the possessor of some sort of
secret, deadly knowledge because of the katas and choreographed movements your sensei taught you. There were
people out there actually learning the correct ways to punch
and kick static targets, targets that were trying to strike back,
to shoot for takedowns and sprawl, actually learning when
and where to apply those methods in a match. It wasn't hard
to see where the new "cool" would lie, and only a blind man
could scoff at the future chanting "TSK! TSK!" in his face.

In December, at the Meadowland Expo Center, Elvis
found himself standing over one of Katz's students, the man
on the bottom struggling to hyperextend Elvis's leg for a submission. But Elvis did what he does best—drop bombs—and
soon Katz's student, a part-time fighter and part-time machin-
ist from Astoria, tapped out. Halfway beneath the ropes and
the tap out went unseen by the referee, so a sea of TSK shirts
went bananas, screaming to the official that he'd missed it.
Katz's student nodded his head, a meek "yes, yes, I tapped
out."

February, the next Reality Fighting, this time in a high
school gymnasium, and Zach was caught under the spell of
the jiu-jitsu magic of his foe, ensorcelled by the string of submission attempts and positional struggles, until he was finally
caught in a triangle choke (a choke done with the legs, the

lower limbs wrapped tight around the neck in the form of an actual triangle). A year later Zach was back in the ring, defeating a last-minute replacement and terminal tomato can, and after winning via that very same submission that cost him the title, Zach, an instructor at one of their Pennsylvania outposts, was suddenly cast from the flock. Gone from their website, gone from their roster. (I never found out why. When I brought it up to his teammates, I was met with shrugs.)

At the same Reality Fighting that saw Zach defeated, Dave came back to demolish an affable grappler, chasing him around with a nonstop barrage of punches until the referee stepped in. But if the night belonged to anyone, it belonged to Laura, the main eventer, the star. It was drama central, and it unfolded when opponent Del Greer failed to make weight— weight a very real factor in the whole victory/defeat equation, an equation where a five- or ten-pound advantage could sometimes negate a conditioning or technique disparity—and the fever pitch was reached when, halfway through the event, promoter Kipp Kollar strode out into the middle of the gymnasium, climbed into the ring, took the microphone, and declared, "Laura has agreed to do it!" The over two thousand spectators in attendance erupted in maniacal glee.

Later on, from my folding chair ringside, I watched the 135-pound TSK fighter approach, ready for battle, a sheen of sweat on her face and her mouth bulging and distorted by the mouthpiece within, a female harder than the polished wood floor she walked upon. Moments later the referee screamed "Go!" and Greer, taller, heavier by seven pounds, black and mean and sporting dreadlocks, shucked off Laura's attempts at securing a takedown and bullied the smaller woman into the corner. Knees and short punches were traded like stocks and bonds. Then it happened, in the latter half of the third and final round, when Laura jumped up and wrapped her legs around Greer's waist, pulling her foe down to the canvas and on top of her. It happened then, when Laura shifted herself and scissored her legs, and their positions were reversed with Laura now on top. Blow after blow after blow, unanswered and ultimately undefended, and the referee stepped in. Laura had won. The people in the bleachers and in chairs on the floor, pure insanity.

Ring of Combat 3, in a recreation center in the sticks of Morristown. The ring was set up in the middle of a dormant ice skating rink, Lou's sparse card a testament to his organization's growing pains. It was June of 2003 and ROC was still struggling to find its legs, but there were championship belts on the line and even then those titles were worth something. For TSK's warriors, the night had mixed results. Dave faced Longo's pupil Luke Cummo, a future finalist on *The Ultimate Fighter*, and came away with his already distorted nose even more mashed. Blood and broken cartilage, and the doctor waived the bout off. Elvis, meanwhile, took on one of Renzo's students and broke his hand punching down on his opponent's big skull. Elvis was the winner via KO but his paw was a mess, a sausage of broken bone encased in leather glove and medical tape, and when I visited his locker room afterward I was shunned as an intruder, as if I was witness to something I shouldn't be (the risk of any post-fight moment when a fighter loses or is injured).

August, ROC 4, in a ballroom at Caesars Atlantic City Casino & Hotel. In the ring in the center, Dave had his rematch with Luke and won after a close, close fight. The crowd, standing around on the carpeted floor, was split between the two camps and caught up in boos and cheers. The announcer paused, the microphone to his mouth, then said that this was Dave's retirement bout. No one was more surprised than Dave himself. He was forty years old at the time.

11

A hard-charger who favored going toe-to-toe over anything else, Dave Tirelli was the first Team Tiger Schulmann representative to test the waters of mixed martial arts competition. The year was 1999 and the event was Xtreme Combat Championships in Clearwater, Florida; the 175-pounder won via armbar. "I've always loved fighting," Dave said, who was almost forty-six years old now and a fifth-degree black belt in the TSMMA system. "It's just my thing." Since that first bout Dave fought once in West Virginia, and then stayed local for the duration of his career, capping his fight record off with the unanimous decision victory over Cummo. What prompted him to step into the ring?

"Way back then, people used to say things about Tiger Schulmann's," Dave said, not quite saying the word *McDojo*, but it was implied and it hung there like an unspoken profanity over our conversation. It was 2009, and we were like two old pals catching up. "So I said, 'Shihan, I'm just not too crazy about what people are saying about this style. I think this is the greatest style. I love it, and I think I want to go out there and compete. I want to prove them wrong. I want to start something here. I think we have something unique. I think we can compete with anyone.' It kind of pissed me off that people would say things about us. People would make fun of us, and I think because of that, and what we did and what I did, we've moved to an unbelievable level. It's one thing that I'm really proud of myself for. I knew what we had was really special and I wanted to step up to the plate. And I really enjoyed it anyway. I was just dying to fight. I started a little too late—I wish [MMA] had been around when I was younger, because it would've been fantastic doing it."

The Cummo fight marked the end of Dave's days of standing and trading strikes in front of a large audience, the coda on a fight résumé he took great pleasure in building. "They pulled a fast one on me and said I wanted to retire, which was the last thing on my mind," he said of the night he was publicly informed of the end of his days as a pugilist. "I wanted to continue fighting. But everyone kept on saying I should do it, and I guess sometimes you have to listen to people. When I fight I like to really fight and bang, and I guess at my age fighting like that wasn't going to be too good on my brain. And I think I'm a much better fighter than I ever was now. I really wish I could go back into the cage. But I guess there's a time when you have to move on to the next thing in life—and that's coaching. That's basically what I do. I work out at our headquarters."

The TSMMA headquarters was where the organization funneled their best. It was where the vast majority of the fight team's blood was spilled. "People from all our facilities come train with us [at the headquarters] and I oversee that," Dave said. "We have classes every single day, in the morning and in the evening. We have adults as well as kids. It's a lot of fun, and I also do private classes. It's a lot of work but I have a lot of guys my age or younger who come to learn with me, and they end up rolling with me or I end up sparring with them, work on their kickboxing—whatever it is."

How did Dave view TSMMA's evolution? "Back then we were learning things, we were learning how to train people at the moment. We didn't have years of experience. I mean, we knew, from Tiger being a world champion in Kyokushinkai, how to get ready for a fight and how to prepare them. But the moves . . . there were so many new moves and counters to moves . . . When we prepare our guys now, I feel we're much more well-rounded. We don't just focus on the strikes and the kicks, we focus on everything. Back then, everything was new. Some of these guys fighting have watched their students or friends fighting in the cage, and it's something exciting. When I did it . . . ," and Dave harkened back to his days blazing the MMA trail.

"For me to find a fight, I had to go on the computer, I had to call all these people, and we used to call all around the country to find someone who would give me a fight. And when you get a fight, then it would be cancelled. It was really difficult to get a fight. These guys can get a fight every couple of months, which is unbelievable, and they're so much more well-prepared. They're training with other people who are fighting professional and amateur. I didn't have so many great people to train with."

He added: "Our fighters are well-rounded and educated. They're sitting there talking about all the books about MMA. 'Have you watched this fight?' That's all they discuss. It's their major passion. Meanwhile, back then I was the one who wanted to do this, I was basically by myself for a while. Now you've got a room packed with amazing fighters."

How does a Tiger Schulmann student end up in the cage? "First of all, everyone wants to fight. Especially when you go to the fights, everyone comes up to you and they say they want to fight right away. So first we have them come down and we have them try out for a class. If they're good, then we

put them in a class and see how they hold out . . . If they can
hold up, if they can hang in there, then we start to get them
into grappling tournaments, boxing tournaments, smokers,
kickboxing, Muay Thai kickboxing. And if they do well there,
amateur MMA. And when they do well there and we think
they're ready to go, we put them into pro."

Dave wasn't shy about extolling the virtues of his team.
He even listed up-and-comers to watch out for, and told a
story of a teenage Louis Gaudinot.

"Let me tell you about Louis Gaudinot," Dave said, his
voice animated and alive and full of the kind of happiness
only fond nostalgia could bring. "I've trained this kid since
he was a little kid—eight or nine or ten, something like that.
I've trained him forever. We were at Mineola [at a Lou
Neglia/Ray Longo amateur kickboxing show], and one of the
other kids dropped out. They said, 'Listen, we need a fighter.'
I had this kid named Paul, and I said, 'Paul, you want to
fight?' He said, 'No, no, I'm just here to watch.' Then Louis
says to me, 'Sensei, I'll fight.' I'm like, alright. He said, 'I don't
have a groin cup or anything.' So we had to find a used groin
cup, we got someone else's sweaty stuff, and the kid went out
there. And it wasn't a fight, it was a war. He won, too. From
right then I knew. I'm proud that he's one of our guys and
one of our instructors."

To hear him tell it, it was clear Dave felt his work was far
from done.

"I want to be so needed at Tiger Schulmann's," he said.
"That's really my goal—being someone who gets our fighters
to another level. I really want to be so involved with our
fighters and teach them things, and see them win with something I taught them. That's really something, because I can't

be in that cage anymore." He added: "I want to build up the headquarters teaching there, and I want to bring a lot more fighters in there. I want to really get a ton more fighters out there."

The MMA veteran, whose 1999 debut forever entrenched his status as an old-schooler, went on to sum up his goals in one sentence: "I want to be an essential and important part of Tiger Schulmann's fight team."

TAP OUT

I first met Kaream in early 2002 at a visit to Katz's Combined Martial Arts gym in Jackson Heights, over a year before the first Underground Combat League event. As the 7 Train rumbled by outside the window, Kaream danced within the confines of a boxing ring, sparring with the kind of confidence reserved only for those sitting comfortably atop the food chain. At a little over six feet tall and around 200 pounds, Kaream had muscles you'd expect on an action hero or member of the X-Men. As fearsome as he looked, Kaream was all respect and smiles when he was done fighting, his man-eating visage replaced by something exceedingly friendly and impossibly approachable.

"Kaream doesn't have a pot to piss in," said Katz, driving home the point that this kid's one and only future lay with MMA. Which was problematic, because the opportunities for an East Coast fighter to earn a paycheck in 2002 were few and far between. The year prior, Kaream fought in two Atlantic City shows, snagging a tournament championship belt and then a loss in an organization that would never again return to New Jersey. That, plus a Garden State underground show here and a small-time show in Virginia there, meant the ultra-talented kickboxer and grappler from the South Bronx had pretty much run the gamut of local revenue-generating options. It was either up, to a spot in the UFC or something almost as big, or it was out the door and back to the streets. You could tell Kaream, his coach Katz, jiu-jitsu trainer Carmine, and the rest of the diverse crew at Combined Martial Arts hoped to God it wasn't the latter. Sit in the audience with the paying customers at any show and you'll overhear someone claiming to be better than everyone in the ring or the cage, or claiming to know someone better than everyone in the ring or the cage, the mythical Manny who can "kick everyone's ass there." Kaream was that myth, flesh and blood and come to life.

Success can be measured in wins or measured in paychecks, or even measured in the number of spectators screaming their lungs out when you rally after taking a beating. Despite a decent record and "the look" (the look promoters and fans are strangely drawn to, that makes someone stick out on a card of tough guys, the "fighter" look), Kaream hadn't really tasted success. But Katz had him under his wing the way an archetypical boxing trainer directs and guides a potential champ, and by June a paying bout was lined up against a salty slugger named Jose at a promotion on Long Island called Vengeance at the Vanderbilt.

Snapshot of Jose: Picture a dilapidated dockside bar, reeking of old fish and stale sea air, and stock that dockside bar with grizzled sailors engaged in the most horrid of brawls—a jaw-breaking, chair-smashing, broken-bottle-across-the-face kind of brawl—until there's but one left standing. If that last man standing looked up and saw Jose walk in the door to give him one more go, that sailor would quit. Unlike those who throw out calculated jabs and hooks and crosses when they fight, when Jose punched he meant it. And though he'd lose that aggressive edge the way angry young men do when they become older men with kids jumping on them calling them "Daddy," in 2002 he was New Jersey pro fighter wielding pure, overwhelming power.

Jose was from the New Jersey–based fight team Pitts Penn, hard-asses all, and he met Kaream in the ring at the Long Island event like an angry locomotive crashing into an overconfident eighteen-wheeler parked complacently on the tracks. Kaream crumbled under the two-fisted onslaught in a minute's time, a pile of human wreckage on the canvas that the referee had to save from further destruction. Afterward, the South Bronx fighter was seen outside the nightclub venue, inconsolable. Success had slipped painfully through the grasp of his fingerless MMA gloves. When I spoke to Carmine about the loss, he just shook his head, expressed his disappointment in Kaream, at the game plan that went out the window because Kaream was too damn cocky and believed no one would, or could, stand and trade strikes with him. Rumor had it that a UFC fighter came to Combined Martial Arts to spar and Kaream's kicks were too much for him to withstand. That all meant nothing now. What happens in a sparring session can sometimes be an indicator of things to come in a real bout, but sometimes not, and Kaream had learned that the hard way at the hands of a badass from the Jersey Shore.

A month later I was in Las Vegas, behind the scenes at a big show called the World Fighting Alliance. The venue was the Hard Rock Hotel & Casino, trendy, cool, glitzy, and fake in the Sin City sort of way, and in the ramp-up to the event, promoter John Lewis was tackling last-minute card changes like a pro, like a man who knew the ins and outs of the business and had heard all the songs and seen all the dances. Right now his main eventer, a massive corrections officer named Marvin, had no opponent. Lewis asked me for suggestions. I described Kaream using colorful words like *killer* and *monster* and stock phrases such as "He likes to bang." But it went nowhere, and though I saw Kaream around every now and then and made a point of shaking his hand, his momentum was gone.

In mixed martial arts, when things get too bleak (a submission hold threatening to break a limb, a choke threatening unconsciousness, a hail of punches you can't get away from, or simply whatever or whenever the situation becomes untenable), you can always tap out. As a general rule there's no shame in it. It just means, "Okay, you got me. You win—this time." This mechanism alone makes for one heck of a safety control. Boxers die from repeated blows to the head in what's tantamount to a contest of who can take the most punishment before brain damage sets in, yet in MMA it's perfectly fine to give up and fight another day. Are there those who refuse to tap out? Of course there are, and they permeate the sport at all levels. But for the most part, at some point or another, whether it's in the gym or in the ring or cage, everyone taps out. That's how it goes.

Vengeance at the Vanderbilt tapped out not long after Kaream fell to Jose, a casualty of shifting political winds, winds that had an indifferent New York State Athletic Commission suddenly giving a shit and enforcing the State's ban on MMA bouts. In Las Vegas, where the sport was sanctioned, the UFC was slowly but surely picking up steam, but in New York events were smothered in the cradle—a cease-and-desist for Vengeance on Long Island, an NYPD visit at a tournament in Brighton Beach—and by 2003 there was nothing. No places to see fights, no places for aspiring fighters to ply their trade. It was either a trip to New Jersey, where MMA was legal and accepted, or spend weekends punching the heavy bag at the gym and picking fights with drunks at bars.

It was in this climate that New York City's illicit fight scene was born, Peter's Underground Combat League the only outlet for an outlaw sport. The lone organization that refused to tap out.

I had to sneak into my first UCL, a veteran reporter of everything from the UFC on down to the sanctioned shows in Bumblefuck, USA. I didn't know Peter yet, wasn't sure if he even wanted press there, but the gravitational pull of no-holds-barred combat within city limits was irresistible like a black hole, a celestial body sucking in all light so that anyone looking at it from a distance could only guess what it was they were looking at. For me, to see it up close was the only option, and I shelled out thirty bucks to play the role of inno-cent spectator and was thankful to be there, thankful that Katz had clued me in and given me the heads-up about this thing going down on a Sunday night in a run-down boxing gym in the Bronx. Word of mouth had brought sixty or so spectators there to see Peter's initial foray into the world of underground fight shows, and I took notes and snapped pic-tures when no one was looking, aware that some kind of momentous occasion was occurring but ignorant of the scope. Gladys, the owner of the gym, worked an electric frying pan behind the front counter, and a fried chicken leg with a slice of white bread could be had for a dollar. Hot sauce was free. I watched Peter scramble for fighters, squeezing out match-ups from people who had no business getting in the ring, but the budding promoter had hired experienced fighter Eddy to be the referee, giving the proceedings a level of professionalism far exceeding what you'd expect from something this far below the radar. At Eddy's insistence, each competitor had to use a mouthpiece, although they could wear track pants, long-sleeved shirts, or even a clown suit if they so chose, and before the first bout he handed me his keys and cell phone to safeguard. The neighborhood was unlike any he and I would have ever considered venturing into for reasons outside of MMA, and if a full-scale riot were to erupt, sure, they probably would've gone after him, the whitest guy in the room by far, but it was no stretch to think I'd be next on the must-shank list. So we stayed close together.

Then Kaream walked in, the fallen pro fighter here simply to see with his own eyes this thing happening two subway stops from his home, and after he and Eddy shared a hug packed with greetings and mutual respect (he and Eddy had fought back in 2001), Peter was all over him begging him to fight. Peter knew him from his accomplishments, knew him as Katz's star player who'd won a tournament in Atlantic City, but didn't know him well enough for Kaream to do him any favors. Only when Peter dangled a carrot in front of him did Kaream relent, the promise of money for books for the upcoming semester at New York City Technical College enough for him to head upstairs to warm up and put on his game face. As Katz wrapped his hands a radiator hissed and dripped nearby, and soon he and Peter met in the squared circle to face each other, the pro fighter in Lycra shorts and the promoter in his blue judo uniform. Kaream needed three minutes and forty seconds to put Peter on his back and torque the judoka's arm until it popped. That was it. The first UCL was one for the books.

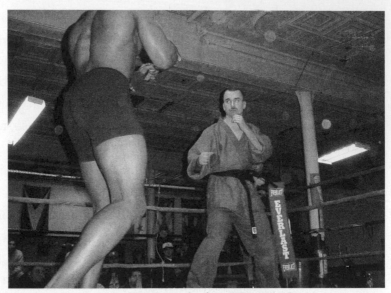

Peter vs. Kaream at the first UCL. (*Jim Genia*)

Back upstairs I stuck a tape recorder in Kaream's face. Post-fight and more often than not you get canned responses, variations on "He was a tough opponent" or "It just wasn't my night" or "Blah-blah-blah," but sometimes you get nuggets of truth, and Kaream talked about wanting to show his fellow South Bronxers what a real mixed martial arts competitor was all about. If things had gone as planned, if Jose had not proven to be too much of a mauler and if the World Fighting Alliance, when it was flying in fighters from as far away as Brazil and Holland, had given him a shot, maybe this conversation would've been taking place somewhere distant and a whole hell of a lot ritzier, like in a pristine Vegas hotel lobby or in the underbelly of the MGM Grand Garden Arena. But no, we were there, now, within the confines of a filthy locker room in a filthy boxing gym, a gym where Clubber Lang could have trained before he put the hurting on Rocky, and when Kaream talked about the streets and doing right by its denizens, I believed him. At this point he was no longer with Katz and Carmine and the crew at Combined Martial Arts anymore. He had jumped from school to school like a wayward and delinquent child, but tonight he had proved to himself that this part of him—the trained and skilled fighter part—was still very, very real.

Slowly the crowd filtered out, Peter along with it, heading to the emergency room for an X-ray and a sling. I got his number from Katz and called him days later, no longer anonymous thanks to the print I had churned out on his behalf (we'd meet in person at an unsanctioned show in New Jersey months later, in the hallway of a middle school while wars raged in a ring set up in the gymnasium). He claimed his motivation for doing an underground show was to create an outlet where he could fight but that he was pleased with the end result. "I was happy," said Peter. "Kaream Ellington saved my show."

December, and this time around New York City's lone underground fight show was in Queens, at Katz's gym. You could put your hand on the canvas of the boxing ring and not fear contracting hepatitis, and you'd be hard-pressed to find duct tape on any of the hanging heavy bags or exercise equipment. Once again Peter had assembled a motley crew for this, his fourth UCL, and when it was time for fists to fly, the metal front gate was pulled down and the glass façade covered with paper. In folding chairs the audience sat, watching as a rough-around-the-edges kid from the Bronx named Richie Torres laid down the law but submitted to a leglock, as a Nigerian-born heavyweight kung fu fighter knocked the mouthpiece out of a wrestler's mouth (it went flying over my head and hit the wall, coming to rest on the floor and lying there like a cursed souvenir no one wanted to touch). The Nigerian lost after delivering nonstop punishment to his foe, the victim of first-time jitters and exhaustion, and when he returned to the curtained-off area in back he vomited all over the place. Then it was Kaream's turn. His opponent was Empire State Games Greco-Roman wrestling champ Bryan, 335 pounds to Kaream's 200, making his debut but scary and built like the villain the Juggernaut sans big, domed helmet. The two faced each other, and in that split second before the rush of combat you could almost hear the crowd, 150 strong, inhale deeply and hold it in.

When the Unified Rules were put in place, weight classes had already been adopted to prevent these types of freak show match-ups, and no athletic commission in the country would've approved of a poundage difference this great. To see someone like Kaream take on someone like Bryan would've required a passport and a plane ticket to Japan or Brazil, not a subway ride to Queens. But here it was, David versus Goliath in mixed martial arts proportions, and it was every kind of spectacle that made the earliest incarnations of the sport fodder for imaginations and newsreels alike.

Peter, acting as referee in jeans, sweatshirt, and socks, yelled for them to begin and Bryan lumbered forward, picking Kaream up and throwing him down. For the next seven minutes the bigger man dropped fists and tried to grab an arm and twist, while beneath, Kaream covered up and squirmed and kept it competitive with elbows and knees to wherever he could land them—nearly smothered by Bryan's bulk but clearly in the game. And slowly, everyone in attendance began to realize that this battle being witnessed, between the monstrous wrestler and the MMA veteran from the streets, was far from the destruction their respective sizes would've normally dictated. As Kaream finally escaped from the bottom to roll Bryan over and rain down bombs, forcing the spent giant to tap out, the crowd's excited yelling and applause was unprecedented.

Afterward, Kaream was awash with strangers congratulating him, all of them inspired by his effort and performance and the fact that, no matter what, no matter how frightening and massive and large and in charge Bryan was, Kaream did not falter. (An older gentleman, possibly someone's dad, made a point of shaking Kaream's hand and saying, evenly, "Holy shit.") I smiled and couldn't help but think that this version of David nailing Goliath with a stone right between the eyes was the true essence of mixed martial arts and the *budo* side of martial arts. Again I stuck a tape recorder into his face, and this time around, when he talked of the bout and the "patience, perseverance, and respect for your opponent" needed to win, I knew that really, on some level, he was talking about himself. "I just had to be patient and wait for the right opportunity," he said. "But I was properly prepared and did my thing."

Like all UCL competitors he was paid nothing for his underground fight, but for Kaream, the payoff was huge.

11

In late 2004, a group of fighters possessing various degrees of sub-UFC experience were sequestered in a house in Las Vegas, cut off from society and forced to face each other in elimination bouts that would culminate in a live broadcast on SpikeTV. This was *The Ultimate Fighter*, the first season of the reality series that brought a glimpse of MMA to more households than ever before and made the sport into a popular, viable industry. At the time, hardcore fans and industry insiders knew bits and pieces of what was going on, and right before the show was to air, UFC president Dana White himself made an impassioned plea on mixedmartialarts.com (the digital epicenter for MMA knowledge, both real and imagined) for hardcores to tune in. They did, as did millions upon millions of other viewers, and TUF was suddenly a star-making vehicle for hopeful fighters.

Outside a Brazilian Jiu-Jitsu academy in Midtown Manhattan at 5:00 A.M., in the predawn darkness and amidst the usual early-morning city sounds (speeding taxis, the maws of garbage trucks groaning and gobbling trash, the occasional car horn resonating off buildings), I saw Kaream and his girlfriend, Jacqueline. Like the passengers in the cab of the pickup truck idling nearby, or the lone men huddled near the academy entrance, Kaream was there for an open casting call. Tryouts, really, for the *Ultimate Fighter*'s second season. His girlfriend, a big white girl with an apprehensive smile, was there to give him support. This morning, Dana White himself would watch as scores of pugilistic hopefuls grappled and hit focus pads and did their best to shine within the confines of a few minutes, minutes that could be worth a lifetime of change and fame and maybe even fortune, or, for the vast majority who would show up, nothing, no change at all. Kaream, Jacqueline, the men huddled by the entrance, the passengers in the idling pickup truck, and myself, we all headed inside, down the stairs to the basement area Renzo had converted into one of the finest Brazilian Jiu-Jitsu schools in the world, blue wall-to-wall mats and a boxing ring and some hanging heavy bags as the scenery. A producer from SpikeTV was already there, as well as a camera crew for a local TV station, a fighter who flew in from San Jose, California, a fighter who drove up from Atlanta, from North Carolina, from Canada.

"We're looking for guys that are well-rounded mixed martial artists," said Dana White, clipboard in hand and flanked by UFC fighter Matt Serra and trainer Ray Longo. "We're looking for guys that are funny, that have great TV personalities," and with that, fighters were paired up and put through their paces, some of them snagging submissions and some of them tapping out, the hungriest and most skilled edging slightly closer to that coveted future in the Octagon. The boxer from Gleason's Gym succumbed to a choke and disappeared. A heavyweight in a judo uniform, out of place among the tattooed warriors in fight shorts, tapped out and disappeared. But the atmosphere was less a shark tank and more a

Kaream (*on his back*) at the tryouts for "The Ultimate Fighter." (*Jim Genia*)

fraternity of brothers where, if you belonged (because you had been toiling and paying your dues and playing the game), you were respected. Did it matter that some poseur chum was eaten along the way?

Kaream locked up with a goateed heavyweight in a white cotton wife beater, stalemating but making it to the next round, to the striking portion of the tryouts where it was all about Longo holding pads while a sequence of numbers was called out, each number representing a type of punch and each fighter doing his best to look like a beast. Then, before the final stage of the process, the brief interview with the big cheese, Dana White dropped the bomb that ended it for Kaream: everyone with a criminal record had to go, and if they didn't now, the vetting process would get them booted regardless. Hit show notwithstanding, this was still television. Bad apples need not apply.

Kaream stammered, perhaps hoping for some sort of exception and bending of the rules, but Dana White waved him off. I had only seen Kaream within the context of MMA, at shows and at gyms, yet I knew he was troubled, that life in the real world had often come at him with varying levels of suck and not all of it of his own making. And I knew that this lost chance was the biggest incursion the streets had had in his future within the realm of mixed martial arts.

Kaream and his girlfriend left in defeat.

The Mixed Fighting Championship debuted in Atlantic City as a huge international affair one step below the UFC in size and prestige, and a year after its inception outrageous fighter salaries and dismal attendance had money flying out the window—which had the matchmaker scrambling for local fighters who would sell tickets. By then he had wised up and

signed Eddie Alvarez, who was famous for being both exciting to watch and attracting busloads of fans from nearby
Philly. But the matchmaker needed more lest his Russian
investors pull out and the MFC crash and burn. He scoured
New York, New Jersey, and Connecticut, plucking from inac-
tivity brawlers and star attractions alike. In the span of a few
months, the MFC went from sinking ship to vessel just taking
on water to boat very much afloat. His fight cards went from
UFC outcasts and almost-but-not-quites, whom no one would
buy a ticket to see, to popular Tri-State area studs taking on
each other, taking on Russians, taking on Japanese fighters.
At MFC 3, a Garden State underground show veteran fought
a Brazilian. At MFC 4, a Connecticut school teacher was
paired up against a huge-fisted Russian. At that same show,
salty slugger Jose from New Jersey put his New England
opponent to sleep with a choke. And in June 2006, Kaream
was given a fight against an experienced 196-pound UFC and
Pride Fighting Championships veteran named Kenichi
Yamamoto.

Kaream approached me after a UCL, two months before
this June bout and next possible big break. Around us, the
crowd within the boxing gym was shuffling out, Richie Torres
congratulated by his friends for winning, Emerson Souza congratulated by his students for defeating Angel Ortiz. Kaream
informed me that his girlfriend was pregnant. I laughed,
hugged him, and patted him heartily on the back. He grinned
in return, a wide smile full of white teeth, apparently very
happy about it as well.

With MFC contract in hand, signed and full of hope and
promising a decent-sized paycheck, Kaream knew that he
needed to train hard. Watch the sport long enough and you
see patterns of who does what best and how they do it, little

things like the ways a Brazilian Jiu-Jitsu specialist is different
from a Japanese jujitsu specialist, how they transition to their
finishing holds, and especially the tendencies of judoka and
wrestlers and all manner of men who gravitate toward grabbing, throwing, twisting, and choking, all of them working
whatever mojo they can. Yamamoto was Japanese and they
were famous for a style of grappling heavy on leglock submissions. For Kaream to be fully prepared, he had to train to
counter them. But train in what?

The answer was sambo, Russia's version of judo, which
is big on leglocks and ankle locks in all shapes and sizes. In
the Land of the Rising Sun, before the UFC gave Brazilian Jiu-
Jitsu global exposure, skilled grapplers had their DNA coded
with moves from sambo, judo, Japanese pro-wrestling (it's for
real over there), and catch-wrestling. Someone like Kenichi
would have had ample opportunity to study the myriad ways
of twisting and tearing apart an opponent's medial collateral
ligament, anterior cruciate ligament, and patellar tendon. But
in the Big Apple, circa 2006, the best at leglocks were the city's
high-level Brazilian Jiu-Jitsu practitioners, tucked away in a
basement academy near Penn Station, and Sambo Steve, an
instructor who ran a school near Times Square. It was Sambo
Steve who took charge of Kaream's grappling training, and
over the next two months the fallen pro fighter, who had
found career rejuvenation after his brief flirtation with New
York City's underground circuit, made the most of it.

Atlantic City's Boardwalk Hall's smaller Adrian Phillips
Ballroom was packed with over 2,200 people (a good-sized
crowd) for the June MFC, an event featuring superstar Eddie
Alvarez, four top female fighters, a slew of foreigners, and, of
course, Kaream. I ran into Jeff Sherwood ringside, hefty and
jovial and towing a suitcase on wheels packed with lenses

and cameras—things you'd expect from a sports shooter and the founder of top MMA news website Sherdog.com. "Is Alvarez really that good?" he asked me, for Sherwood would be snapping pics of the action here. I told him yes, Alvarez was that good, but he shrugged and put all his imaginary chips on Alvarez's opponent, a UFC veteran named Derrick. Meanwhile, a reporter and photographer duo from the *New York Times* showed up, wide-eyed and curious, and soon the bouts were underway.

I took my seat, just inches from Kaream's corner, and when it was his turn to step into the ring I watched as he approached from backstage, intent and focused, Sambo Steve a few steps behind. Kaream gave me a quick bow of his head—no smile, all business—and climbed the wooden steps, past the ropes, hopping on one foot then the other, glancing at his opponent in the opposite corner before turning back to face his corner men. Sambo Steve was giving him last-minute instructions, but if Kaream heard any of it I couldn't tell. I couldn't even discern it myself, my heart racing and my mind full of hope that this man with a kid on the way, who deserved a break and a chance to get off the streets, that he didn't get smashed in front of Sherwood and the *New York Times*. He really, really needed this, and the world deserved to know that Kaream was more than capable of kicking serious butt.

The referee signaled for them to go and it was on, and from the outset it was clear the two were evenly matched kickboxers. But mixed into the exchange of punches and kicks was a suplex, a wrestling technique that Kaream utilized to launch Yamamoto over his head and onto the canvas (the crowd let out a loud "ooooh!"), and right then and there, after a scramble for position, Kaream wound up on his back with his legs up and the Japanese fighter grabbed one of the appendages and fell backward into a leglock. Tomorrow, the front page *New York Times* article would feature a photo of female fighters Amanda Bucker and Shanya Bazsler grappling near the ropes, and Sherwood would raise his eyebrows and mouth an exclamation to me when Alvarez knocked Derrick out in a minute and one second, but right now, it was all about Kaream countering the submission perfectly by rising up, pulling his foot free, and punching down. (Sambo Steve screamed his approval so loud I feared he would go into cardiac arrest.) Yamamoto got back to his feet and attempted a bent-armlock, and Kaream answered with knees, a stream of them to Yamamoto's head that stunned him, forcing him back down to the canvas, defenseless, and prompting the referee to step in. Kaream was victorious.

Afterward, Kaream, now in his regular clothes, found me ringside. And he gave me a big, meaningful hug.

III

I don't pretend to know the demons that can drive a man from the brink of success to the depths of defeat, suffice to say that Kaream had them, and for whatever reason, they managed to keep him down. After that June MFC, billionaire Calvin Ayre flushed the organization with cash and turned it into BodogFIGHT, a promotion heralded as the one true competitor to the UFC but in reality just a way for the matchmaker to spend ridiculous amounts of Ayre's money. Kaream was among the twenty fighters flown down to a private compound in Costa Rica, paired up against each other for bouts that would comprise a television program intended to be the

next best thing to the *Ultimate Fighter* show, and in a ring
erected within a jungle setting, Kaream fought unprepared.
He was submitted in the second round, in a match that would
air months later on a Christian-based cable network barely
seen by anyone who would care. I learned this when Kaream
called to tell me that Jacqueline, now his wife, had given birth
to his son, and though from speaking with Sambo Steve I
knew that Kaream hadn't been training ("I don't know, man.
He's disappeared."), I still harbored hope that things would
work out for the warrior from the South Bronx. I congratulated him on his son and wished him, truly wished him, all
the best. One last bout on his contract and Kaream was sent to
Tokyo, Japan, the sole American on an event that for him
ended with a submission defeat in just over two minutes.
Kaream didn't compete in MMA again.

On November 7th, 2007, his wife was found murdered
outside a six-floor apartment building. According to police
reports her throat was slit and she was stabbed multiple times
before being thrown off the roof of a well-known drug location. She had been living in a women's shelter in Manhattan
with Kaream's toddler, struggling. Jacqueline was twenty-one
years old.

Kaream called me, his voice grim and sapped of life. It
had been over a year since we last spoke, and his absence had
left all within the scene to assume that whatever called him
back to the streets had called him back for good, assumptions
painful and saddening for those who had hoped this troubled
soul would be different. I expressed my condolences, more
heartfelt than my hugs and best wishes ever were, and
Kaream asked if I knew of any leads. Mixed martial arts was
his greatest source of success; he needed money now to raise

his son, as the lone parent more so than before. I promised to put his name back out there, and he followed up with an e-mail, an impassioned plea to every promoter, reporter, and news outlet that would listen. The e-mail read:

"Hi. This is Kaream Ellington. My wife, Jacqueline Irizarry, was murdered November 7th and I now must raise my son alone. I now must provide for my son and mixed martial arts is what has provided the most helpful income. In the past, I have made the mistake of allowing myself to become absorbed into the very things that destroyed my community and have now taken the love of my life and left my son without a mother. Law enforcement is conducting an investigation into who did this as our families are mourning. Throughout my career, and my life, Jacqueline supported me and wanted the best for me and our son. I thank you for all the help, opportunities, and inspiration. Jacqueline always told me to never quit MMA, just give it all I've got. I will honor her wishes until I see her again."

Kaream was put on the card for a Combat at the Capitale kickboxing-only event in January, just months later, but he lost via TKO in the third round.

I got a text from Peter asking me to be at Katz's school in Astoria—not for a UCL, but for an on-camera interview for a documentary on the underground promotion. When I arrived Katz was sitting before the camera, answering questions in his usual friendly but fast-talking manner, and soon I was before the camera. When I was done I chatted with Peter. Katz joined us. We reminisced about everything, from Peter's events to the fighters who had lived and (figuratively) died in the ring, and of course Kaream came up.

"He's in jail," said Katz, and the details included a weapons possession charge, failed efforts at trying to visit Kaream at Central Booking, and the likelihood that Kaream would be facing a lengthy incarceration.

Peter and I shook our heads at the news, three shades of disappointment and "Damn. Seriously, damn," and an unspoken rhetorical question hung in the air.

Had Kaream finally tapped out?

LYMAN

Lyman stepped into the ring at ROC 9 in 2005 a neophyte, but his TSK training, and the smoldering embers of seething emotion just below the surface of his thousand-yard stare, were enough to enable him to wage a winning war against his Pitts Penn-trained foe. At that event—at the Asbury Park Convention Hall, an Arctic hell in the cool fall night—teammate Uriah made his debut as well, a forty-four-second mugging of the kneeing and punching variety. Like fine wines, Lyman and Uriah had been kept in the cellar of TSK headquarters, fermenting and aging until they had attained perfection, and if Dave and Elvis and Laura were trailblazers and prototypes, Lyman and Uriah were the fruits of their organization's momentous labors and a process refined and refined again until what was left was "simply smashing" in the purest, most combative sense of the phrase.

Ring of Combat 10, and this time around the venue was the Showroom in the Tropicana. Gone now are the days of ice rinks, shiver-inducing drafts, and sweaters, the economics of it all such that Lou was no longer a nomadic promoter, instead under contract with a casino that believed firmly in the ability of MMA to attract potential gamblers. One more show in a ballroom in Caesars and then it was the Tropicana from then on, the Tropicana where Lyman had his second fight, a gutsy, anger-fueled performance that began with his hand fracturing from the first punch he threw in the opening round and his opponent, now blissfully unconscious thanks to his last punch in the second round, sailing through the ropes. When referee Big Dan pulled Lyman away the TSK fighter resisted, snarling like a frenzied Rottweiler unwilling or unable to back down. There was no mistaking that he wanted to keep going.

Laura was soon gone from the TSK, gone from fighting as well, leaving competition the number-one female fighter in the world to marry a Brazilian black belt with a jiu-jitsu school in Newark. Then there was Elvis. ROC 10 was Elvis's swan song, a last hurrah that showcased his ability to unleash pure, destructive fury. Seventeen seconds of bombs and Christian, an instructor at the Fighthouse and my friend, was unconscious, Christian's time spent sparring with amateur boxers at Katz's gym in preparation failing to stack up to Elvis's time spent sparring with pro boxers at TSK headquarters. But time had made Elvis older, older than when he and his team had begun their journey, and while it is widely accepted that power is the last thing to go, it was getting tougher and tougher for the stocky Hispanic fighter to cut weight. When he had won the belt years before it was at 160 pounds; he was 173 for Christian, and pounds over the agreed-upon limit. And then there was the saga of his constantly breaking hand. "It kind of fractured when I hit him with the last punch," Elvis said to me afterward, the warmth and optimism in his voice a world away from the chill in the locker room at ROC 3. "It's not as broken as the last time so recovery shouldn't be as long," he said. "It's just a small break, nothing major. Last time I had to get pins in there. This time it's just a little break." But that was it. Elvis, the last of Tiger Schulmann's first wave of MMA competitors, was done, the baton passed. Now it was time for Lyman, for a pugnacious ex-wrestler from Long Island named Rich, for a world-class kickboxer named Uriah, and for an army of young bloods flooding the amateur leagues.

The sport was hot now, hotter than ever thanks to the *Ultimate Fighter*, and the entire industry was flush with moneymen looking to invest, promises and ideas and optimism floating around like balloons at a child's second birthday party. So Lou orchestrated his "Tournament of Champions," and when the eight men in each of four weight divisions was whittled down to one over the course of three events, ROC would have its very own tried and true bad asses supreme. Tiger Schulmann fielded Rich at lightweight (155 pounds) and Dominic at welterweight (170 pounds). Their opponents were K-Rod and Jay.

Snapshot of K-Rod: tall, skinny, tattooed K-Rod (real name: Kevin Roddy) looks like he should be toting around a surfboard or packing a bong in the back of a skateboard repair shop. But a concise jiu-jitsu game has made him dangerous—more dangerous than you'd expect from someone so happy-go-lucky and unimposing—and as Jersey Shore pro fighters go, few can match his record in sheer number of fights. By 2010 K-Rod's a part-time competitor, paired up against up-and-comers to teach them to never make mistakes (a mistake and he'll hyperextend your arm or use his legs to choke you out), but in 2006 he's hungry, and considered one of the Northeast's best.

ROC 12, the Tournament of Champions opening round, and I was asked to put down the pad and pencil and don a headset, a journalist turned color commentator, the "in the know" person to veteran sportscaster Bruce Beck's play-by-play for the delayed pay-per-view showing. In the ring Rich dodged everything K-Rod threw at him, Rich the underdog by far when his comparative fight experience was taken into account, but he was escaping, escaping the triangle chokes and armbars, avoiding trouble into the third frame. Between rounds and Rich was on a stool, catching his breath as Tiger Schulmann instructed and advised, throwing combinations in the air to demonstrate, and then came the final sequence, when the lanky K-Rod was caught standing in front of him, a grappler playing a striker's game. Rich, a strong counter-puncher with vicious, evil hand speed, was most definitely a striker. The Jersey Shore fighter went down and Rich was victorious.

Dominic wasn't quite so lucky. Straddling the line between cocky and confident, full of white-hot emotion, he squared off against Jay, Jay an ex-wrestler with an innate sense of timing, a trait that somehow enabled him to knock out other wrestlers with uncanny regularity. Dominic wound up flat on his back near the ropes, out cold in a scant thirty-eight seconds, and when he came to he stormed off to the locker rooms downstairs, cursing, fuming, not even allowing the doctors near to check him out (behavior that gets him temporarily suspended by the athletic commission). He never stepped into the ring again.

Two months later, Lyman returned to face a Renzo Gracie black belt at World's Best Fighter, his molded features and pinpoint striking turning the bout into a caricature of "normal man versus superhero." World's Best Fighter was a one-off event, another prime example of someone smelling big returns on investments but finding the reality of the bouquet not quite as fragrant. Only Lou's ROC persevered, and six weeks later it was the second round of the Tournament of Champions.

When Rich climbed into the ring at ROC 13, he bore upon his shoulders the hopes of his organization winning the biggest regional tournament around, and when he tapped to a choke in a minute and a half, it was as if he had failed more than just himself and his teammates, but in fact let down the entire world. (He didn't. It was only a fight and he was far and away the underdog.) He left the ring defeated that night, a black cloud stuck hovering just above his head, and when he returned at ROC 15 that black cloud remained, a gypsy curse he couldn't seem to shake (I was told he no longer trained like he used to—the death knell for anyone serious about fighting). Rich fell to a heavy-handed judo player, came back to get submitted by Doug at ROC 17, and then he was done.

Lyman's career, however, was headed in the other direction. Arrive early at a show and you shook hands with people you would see repeatedly but only once a month or so, maybe took your warm greeting from Big Dan and Kevin Mulhall (ultra-experienced Kevin, the other half of the New Jersey Star Refereeing Dynamic Duo), maybe asked Katz or Carmine what was new and checked with Lembo about which fight was off because someone flaked out or tested positive for hepatitis, and in the midst of the ritual would come the names, uttered with curiosity mixed with cautious respect, the who's who of possible up-and-comers and future stars. "What do you know about so-and-so?" or "I heard so-and-so is fighting tonight. Is he really that good?" After three dominant performances Lyman's name had begun to fill in that blank, knowledge of him and his potential the new currency, like knowing what a force Randy Couture would become or how Forrest Griffin was ultra-experienced and tough before he ever set foot in the *Ultimate Fighter* house. Talk to any TSKer or Shihan himself and they would all extol the virtues of their fighter from Spanish Harlem, but the ring doesn't lie, and there, for all to see, emerged ever so slowly the truth.

At ROC 14 Lyman had his fourth bout, against Erik, a six-foot-five striker from upstate New York, and they danced an intricate dance of timing and well-placed, well-thought-out blows until Erik threw a kick that Lyman blocked with an elbow. The round ended, the opening round of what promised to be a contest of patience and strategy, and from my seat I caught a glimpse of Erik's foot. It was distorted, expanding like a horrific kind of balloon, and though Erik waved off his corner men and tried his best to dismiss the approaching doctors, it was clear that within that foot were smashed bones, smashed and fractured and broken, causing the appendage to swell. Erik could no longer walk. The bout was over.

Two months from that victory and Lyman was back, on the undercard of a doomed mega-show in Atlantic City's Boardwalk Hall called Cage Fury Fighting Championship, part of the lead-in for the Kimbo Slice versus Ray Mercer main event. The matchmaker had wisely put every local big ticket seller he could on the roster, and Lyman got to face Doug. I saw Lyman the day before at the weigh-ins, held at a nightclub in Atlantic City, and the TSK rep was spent from cutting weight, the process involving driving down from New York City with the windows up and the heat on full blast until he was down to 174 pounds. In the nightclub, everyone even tangentially related to Renzo's team sat in one section, Kimbo and his people in another, while K-Rod joked and his Lithuanian ex-rugby player opponent smiled in silence. At the event the next day, Gregor Gracie would win and K-Rod would tap to an armbar, and two teams would storm the cage when one fighter pushed an opposing trainer after a match (something about a girl?). Frankie the future UFCer was standing in jeans and T-shirt with his mates, his fists clenched against a swarm of fighters from Ricardo Almeida's. But first there was Lyman, who for all three rounds took Doug down, muscled him to the edge of the cage, and ground and pounded him with the finality of a judge meting out capital justice.

Outside the cage, Lyman was beginning to fray around the edges. There was talk of turmoil at home, issues with his sister threatening to alter the vector of his determined climb, but within the cage he was a monster, and a turning point was coming, a point where all his efforts would translate into accolades and money—the oft-sought-after payoff.

The International Fight League returned to New Jersey after traipsing around the country to lose money, and in one of its last gasps it cobbled together an event at the Izod Center in East Rutherford and put Lyman and teammate Nissim on the undercard. The cornerstone of the IFL had been setting its contrived teams against each other, a notion that took off about as well as New Coke and the Edsel (at its heart MMA is an individual sport and not a team sport), and at the sub-national level fans only care about local fighters. But this IFL had a team fielded by Renzo, and in the prelims, two of Tiger Schulmann's most popular fighters turned the venue into a madhouse. Nissim fell to a Ricardo Almeida-trained fighter named Dante, a third-round TKO loss involving Dante sitting on Nissim's chest and raining down fists, yet Lyman got the job done. Like a choir on crystal meth, the Tiger Schulmann contingent chanted "TSK! TSK!"—a combination mantra and battle cry—and throughout, Lyman ran the gamut of tech-

Peter focusing on his impending bout.

Peter fighting Kirkland.

Kirkland on top of James.

James (*right*) knocking Kirkland out with a spectacular kick.

Kirkland knocked out.

Team Funaro celebrating their win.

Chris (*right*) throwing a punch at Mike.

Mike kicking Chris while he's down.

The New Generation karate coaches instructing from ringside.

Marwin on top of Harley Flanagan.

Harley Flanagan of the Cro-Mags.

Slugfest in the Bronx.

Chris and Marwin shaking hands before their fight.

Kevin (*left*) warming up with Peter.

Kevin landing a left.

Kevin (*right*) pounding on Xavier.

Kevin (*left*) being congratulated by his foe.

Irish kid knocked out in Brooklyn.

Chris on top of Lionheart.

Chris going for a takedown against the ropes.

Chaz (*left*) fighting with one eye.

Chaz victorious.

Chaz being interviewed by Fox 5 News after his win.

Kirkland pounding Joe.

Jerry (*in red*) checking out Kirkland's eye.

Kirkland and Joe after their battle.

Adam (*in black*) about to mix it up.

Adam taking a knee to the midsection.

Arjang throwing a kick.

Lyman (*right*) punching at World's Best Fighter.

Lyman victorious at World's Best Fighter.

Fedor Emelianenko at TSK.

Kenneth (*left*) about to unleash hell.

Kimbo at the EliteXC weigh-ins in Florida.

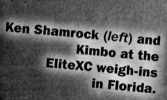

Ken Shamrock (*left*) and Kimbo at the EliteXC weigh-ins in Florida.

Kimbo after beating Ray Mercer.

Steve DeAngelis warming up.

"The Story" getting his hands wrapped.

niques against his foe, first throwing strikes, then transition-
ing to grappling and hunting for a choke, then back to trading
punches. He won by unanimous decision, and from my perch
in press row I could almost see Lyman exhale a monumental
sigh of relief from the depths of his very soul.

Seven months passed and it was ROC 18, and Lyman
seemed relaxed, even well-rested, against Alexis, a man who
defeated Nissim the year before. The classic Jekyll and Hyde,
Alexis was nice between fights and furious when in the
middle of one, and his boxing and wrestling made for one
tough son-of-a-bitch in combat. But Lyman picked him apart,
pausing only when Alexis switched stances midway through
to throw wild, unorthodox strikes. Like a Terminator, Lyman
analyzed, adjusted, and when time ran out, his arm was
raised in victory.

"Growing up, it was natural for me to become a fighter,
just from the circumstances I've endured," Lyman said. "Just
from the places I've lived in." It was nearly 9:00 P.M. at the
TSMMA Manhattan facility and, after a long day of training
with the fight team in New Jersey and teaching students here,
his demeanor spoke of the relaxation and fatigue only the
rigors of extreme exertion could bring. "I've lived in a pretty
tough area, pretty tough neighborhood," he said. "It was like
a drug-dealing, gun-toting, gangbanging type of neighborhood. I felt like, just from that alone, early on I had to establish myself as a fighter both mentally and physically. I felt like
I had to do that just to survive. The same thing applied
throughout high school. I always had to fight for everything.
Growing up I was in a lot of fights and altercations with
people. Aside from that, I joined military school at one point
and started training in martial arts. When I got into it, it was

something that absorbed me right away. The whole combative sports, there was something to it that tested me as an individual and as a person. After that, what I was going to do was go into the marines. But considering how much I got into the combative sports, I decided to forget about that. I needed money. I was struggling to survive. I had two sisters to take care of, I had my mother whom I was helping support. I needed the money, so I felt like, 'This is it. This is where my future is.'"

Lyman's daily regimen included a three- to four-hour workout with the fight team, where he, along with a host of other aspiring TSMMA amateurs and pros were put through the Ninth Level of Hell via sparring, plyometrics, calisthenics, rope climbing, and other sport-specific exercises. From 3:00 P.M. he punched the clock as an instructor. His teaching schedule remained the same regardless of whether or not he had a fight scheduled, and his training intensity stayed in a constant high-octane fifth gear no matter what. The word *dedication* didn't even come close.

It did, however, come at a cost. Time and again fighters would say that most of the fight was fought in the preparation, and few rivaled Lyman's extreme levels of preparation. With prodding he revealed a rough spot that arose when his strict regimen began to take its toll. "I guess every fighter has his moment of weakness, of complete and utter deterioration, both mentally and physically," he said. "I had that one time where I was training so much. One of the problems I have is insomnia—two or three hours a night is considered a good night. I reached a point where I was just physically breaking down. I was just training with all these injuries. I was going in sick and I caught pneumonia. Giving 100 percent of myself all the time became excruciating. It got to the point where I was training sick, I was training broken, I was training every way possible. My mother, it brought tears to her eyes to see what condition I was training in. I came to the school one time after one of my plyometrics training sessions, and I went into the back office, turned the lights off, and secluded myself in darkness. And I just broke down. I said to myself, 'This is too much. This is a lot for a normal human being to go through.' There was just so much weight on my shoulders mentally and physically . . . It felt like a dehumanizing process. It got to a point where afterward I realized it was a turning point, like shedding skin, and when I left that room I felt like I had left that weakness in that room. I went out there and fought (against Erik, Doug, and his opponent in the IFL) and I proved to myself that no matter the adversity, I will overcome it.

"Going into my first fight I didn't know exactly what to expect," said Lyman, reflecting on what it was like at ROC 9. "I guess overall, the aura that was surrounding my first fight was a sense of detachment—a lack of expectations. I'm not going to say I was nervous for the fight, because I wasn't, but then again I didn't know what to expect going into the fight. I just felt the most important thing that was crucial for the fight was to prepare myself as much as possible. Just train and train my hardest and know that I'm going to be much more well-prepared than my opponent. And considering how much I trained for that first fight, I stepped in there confident."

Whenever he stepped into the ring, the first thing you noticed about him was his conditioning, which was apparent in his impossible physique. The second thing you noticed was his intensity. Third on that list, his confidence. Did he ever feel any doubts? "There's only one part of the fight that I ever doubt myself in," he said. "One little, short moment, one frag-ment of time in which all the possibilities come to mind, and it's on my way to the ring. To me, it's like the longest walk ever. Like a mile long just from the locker room into that ring. You just start thinking, and everything is like tunnel vision, everything gets put into perspective, everything becomes focused into that one moment. All of your training, all of your effort, all of the pain, everything—just channeled into that small, little walk. And you're basically doubting yourself. 'What if this happens? What if that happens?' But once I enter that ring, once I get in there, that switch goes off. My mind gets cleared and I'm ready to go. I look across that ring and know what I have to do."

At this stage in the game Lyman had faced a variety of fighters, from slugger to jiu-jitsu black belt to brawler to tech-nician. I asked who was toughest. "Every opponent I've had has had something different to offer as far as difficulty," he said. "I want to say it was probably my second fight . . . and the reason it seemed hard was I had fractured my hand with the first punch. Therefore, there was a little bit of doubt that I was going to be able to finish that fight, let alone that first round, due to the fact that I'd broken my hand. I went into my corner and didn't even complain about it, didn't say a word, didn't do anything. I was like, 'I've got to go out there and I've got to win.' In that second round I went out there a completely different person. Just from that I feel like maybe he was my toughest opponent."

I pressed further about that second fight, and how Lyman didn't seem to want to stop when Big Dan pulled him off. "It was my first knockout, and on top of that, I felt like I didn't just knock him out, I felt like I had overcome the adversity that I had had in my mind. Going back to that first round, I said to myself, 'How the fuck am I going to finish this first round? How am I going to finish this fight?' And going into that second round and winning it, it was all this emotion and all this anger, everything just kind of came out."

Was there pressure representing Tiger Schulmann's? "There's pressure, but you try to block that out. That's another thing that happens when you step in between those ropes. You confine yourself to just four walls and two corners—yours and your opponent's. And you try to focus on your opponent."

When a fighter makes his way to his corner in between rounds, what transpires is one part cheerleading and one part informational download, the information conveyed based on the analysis of an extra few pairs of eyes. I've seen it up close from ringside, but the perspective of the fighter sitting on that stool for sixty seconds is another animal entirely. I asked about what goes on in Lyman's corner. "Shihan Schulmann is very honest in terms of telling you what the situation is, what's ahead of you, and what you have done so far. He'll tell you if you've lost that round, you've got to pick it up, you've got to do your thing. One thing about my trainer is that he's very good at not just knowing you as a fighter but as a person. So he knows how to get to you—to your mind or heart or whatever the case may be—and he knows how to rile up this thing in you. He knows what to say to set you off, regardless of how bad you might've lost the first round. It's weird. It's like he knows what to say. He tells you what it is you need to win. And he's very perceptive. He looks at things I don't normally look at or things you wouldn't be able to see as a fighter. From an outside perspective, he just tells you what it is you need to do to finish that round. If you're tired, he knows what to do to bring you back up. And you feel con-

fident. When you go back to your corner you feel comfort-
able . . . Every time you go back to your corner you feel like
you're going back to something you can rely on."

I asked Lyman about heroes and if he had them. Most
pointed to fighters they admired, like Couture or the Brazilian
Wanderlei Silva, but he went the other way with it, and the
choice made by the burgeoning superstar with only one
parent spoke volumes. "Inside the sport, Shihan Schulmann,"
he said. "In a way it's funny. He's become like a father to me.
I have that level of trust with him, and that's one of the most
important things you have to establish before you can do anything. Outside of the sport, I want to say my mother. She's
tough. She's not weak-minded. She's a very, very strong
person." What did his mother think of him fighting? "She
loves it. We have this tradition where she slaps me hard
across the face before every fight to wake me up. That's her
way of kissing me almost, usually in the back room a few
hours before a fight.

"I feel like, still, to this day, I'm fairly new to it," Lyman
said. "One of the things I always go into the ring with is a
lack of complacency. I'm never just happy with what I have so
far. I always want better. I'm hungry. I just want to become
the best."

11

No conversation with Lyman was complete without him mentioning his teammates, the youngsters who were raised on
TSK and who, when the organization adapted to the new
sport, were shaped into the sport's newest, most refined athletes. In the midst of Lyman and Rich's professional exploits,
Jimmie and Nick were slogging through the amateur leagues,

racking up wins and earning championship belts, and I tracked them down.

"When I started competing when I was younger I realized that I loved to compete," said Jimmie, a nineteen-year-old 145-pounder who taught at the school in Ramsey. "It was always a thrill to win. If I didn't win, I just thought it was something I'd learn from and take it in for the next one." Jimmie was short, just under five and a half feet tall, but he was fit and his frame carried no excess baggage. He had been with Tiger Schulmann since he was a kid, and had racked up an undefeated record in kickboxing to go with his undefeated record in amateur MMA—eleven bouts in both sports combined. How did he end up competing in mixed martial arts?

"I told Shihan, 'You know, Shihan, when I'm eighteen I want to do MMA fights and stuff like that.' So they found a venue—New Breed Fighters, which is great for any amateur fighters to get experience in—and from there I just kept on going. Since I turned eighteen in June of 2007, I've had a fight in every month of last year."

What was his first taste of MMA combat like? "My first MMA fight was in August [of 2007] against Thiago Carfi; he was a Renzo Gracie kid. I was tearing him up with my hands, and of course I knew he was a grappler, so I stayed up mostly on my feet. We actually ended up on the ground a little bit, and I was beating him on the ground. He wasn't bad, he knew a couple locks, but he just went for the same ones the whole time. I just looked for that whenever we were on the ground. But most of the time I was on my feet, and he would duck down and try to take me down . . . From my first fight that August to this past June, there's a tremendous difference in how I fight and how much better I got."

Did Jimmie believe he was sufficiently prepared for his

first venture into the cage? "I was prepared," he said. "I also did wrestling when I was in high school. One of the things was with Shihan is we're well-rounded. We always work on everything. You see some grappling schools only doing jiu-jitsu, Muay Thai schools only doing Muay Thai—we do everything. But the most important thing that we always focus on is being in shape. When I went into my first fight I felt I was in great shape. I went all three rounds and felt great."

Nick started training at TSK when he was ten, and now the twenty-one-year-old amateur champ could boast an unde-feated record to his students when he taught at the Bay Ridge school. "I was always in tournaments," he said. Nick was smaller than Jimmie, a 135-pound fighter in a world that valued more those much heavier, but he was explosive and absolutely fearless in the cage. "I was always in the Tiger Schulmann tournaments that are held twice a year. I was win-ning those a lot and I just got the itch for it. The UFC became big and Tiger Schulmann's evolved into mixed martial arts, and I just took it on. I fell in love with it from the second I started."

How did his first fight go? "My first MMA fight I was kind of nervous, to tell you the truth. I think everyone is nerv-ous when they get in the ring. I got in there and was a little nervous just with the gloves and no headgear. I'd fought Muay Thai before, but MMA is totally different. So I got in there and the second the bell rang my body relaxed and I started throwing—it was an unbelievable experience. The second I was done I wanted to do it again."

Was he sufficiently prepared? "Oh yeah," Nick said. "I feel like I was definitely prepared for it. I've been prepared for all my fights because Tiger Schulmann's just trains the hell out of everybody. You don't fight unless you train, and if you don't train he's going to pull you from that fight."

At ROC 21 Jimmie went pro, defeating a Brazilian black belt after beating on him for the duration, and at ROC 22 Nick took the plunge and decisioned a wrestler.

Then it was time for Bellator.

Cruise down the highway of history and you'll see the landscape of MMA littered with the still smoldering wrecks of dead promotions, orgs that aimed high but crashed and burned in spectacular style. BodogFIGHT, EliteXC, and the IFL all tried, and for various reasons, failed. So it was that when the idea of the Bellator Fighting Championships—a Latino-centric organization featuring eight-man tournaments across four weight classes—was announced, the news was met with great trepidation. Why would it matter that Bellator weekly events would air on ESPN Deportes? The IFL made it to television, and EliteXC was responsible for breaking the prime-time seal on a major network, but that all meant jack when the reaper knocked on their doors. What difference would it make that Bellator would feature established MMA stars and hungry up-and-comers? BodogFIGHT utilized a similar mixture. Where was it now? No, it would take a lot more to ensure Bellator's success, intangibles like hype and buzz, a kind of magic that only occurs when there's substance to the product and at least the air of someone competent behind the wheel.

In the period of time Bellator went from mere talk to real action, rumors abounded about the missteps, the suffocating fighter contracts, and abrupt staff changes, and none of it was surprising to anyone who had observed the industry for any extended period of time and saw those mistakes made a million times before. But tournaments! Fans love tournaments, from back in the days of the early UFCs when real warriors had to fight three times a night, swimming through a pile of sixteen tough guys until there was only one left standing, and goddamn if you couldn't point to that last man standing as the baddest one of all. Fighters made their own destinies with tournaments. And though they went out of vogue as time passed, the practice survived in Japan, eventually decompressing until each subsequent round took place over the course of a few shows. Such was the case with ROC's Tournament of Champions and such was the case with Bellator, and over ten events, champs at 145, 155, 170, and 185 pounds would emerge.

When Lyman was announced as a participant in the 170-pound tournament, the whispers were that he was one to watch. There were others in the brackets, though, a grizzled UFC veteran here, a skilled Midwestern fighter named Hector there, a slew of voracious newcomers and of course everyone knew that the nature of the beast was such that anything, absolutely anything could happen (an alternate stepped into the last round of UFC 3's tourney back in 1994 and won it all—talk about your long-lasting scars). But Lyman was the Northeast's open secret, and when Bellator's second installment rolled into the neighborhood, his name was the name on the lips of those cheering in the crowd and those scrutinizing from press row.

Mohegan Sun Arena (at Mohegan Sun Casino) in Connecticut, thirteen months after his last fight, and Lyman was backstage, sequestered and watched over by tribal commission officials like all fighters are pre-show. As venues go, Mohegan Sun Arena was one of the nicer ones, and though the commission there was new—an athletic commission a necessary accoutrement for the surrounding big-money casino and its ability to bring in big-money sporting events—and their mistakes sometimes green, it was often a smooth ride for promoters, media, fighters and their camps, and any other parties involved. Often, but not always.

"We're looking for someone from the commission," Tiger Schulmann said to me. It was a few hours before start time and I was near the cage, near my seat in press row, and he was there with his brother Ron. "Lyman hasn't eaten all day and we want to bring him some food, but they won't let us bring anything back there." Vast sections of the crowd were bedecked in TSMMA garb, ready-made frenzies waiting to happen, and I noted how Bellator was smart securing Lyman in that regard, as a dead crowd at a fight show is the bane of good MMA television. I asked Tiger and Ron how Lyman was feeling, how his training had gone and if he was ready. Their words were confident, variations on how much of a monster he was and how he was going to kill. About us, technicians and cameramen, a camera on a boom taking practice runs on overhead shots, and within the cage the announcer was finding his marks and going over his lines. Zack, the photographer, inserted a memory stick into his camera and fiddled with the settings, and in press row laptops sprung to life. Big Dan was there to ref and he and Kevin Mulhall gave me a friendly handshake/hug hybrid.

Then it was showtime, and first up was Jimmie, weighing 136 pounds now and too much, way too much, for his opponent, coming close with submissions and hoisting him up for slams until the third round when, mercifully, Jimmie slipped on the triangle choke and forced the tap out. The partisan audience cheered. Throughout the event, the announcer went through the introductions and post-fight talk twice, once in Spanish and once in English, and when Lyman's video intro came up on the big screen he was shown walking through his gritty upper-Manhattan neighborhood, *"Boricua* to the bone" according to the announcer's description, all the while subtitles translating what Lyman said for the non-Spanish speakers watching. Much was made of how hard he trained, how he did this for his family, and even his mother got screen time.

When Lyman emerged from backstage, madness.

In the cage and they were fighting, Lyman and Hector, and Hector appeared too small and too human, unable to match the 10,000-degree heat bearing down upon him. Lyman took him to the canvas and pounded on him in the first round, kicked him in the head in the second round, and twisted out of a precarious position to put Hector to sleep with a choke. Lyman was moving on to the semi-finals.

Around me, press row muttered a collective "Jesus."

A month later and Lyman was facing a skinny, overmatched fighter named Jorge in Chicago. There was no Team Tiger Schulmann contingent this time around to turn the venue into a monstrous pep rally, but it didn't matter; Lyman matched Jorge's wild punches with tight ones of his own, and when Jorge wound up cut above the eye, it was all over.

June 12th, 2009, and I was at ROC 25 in New Jersey, the event held the same night as Bellator's welterweight final. Before me, in the cage (ROC had now switched from a ring to a cage), green-haired demon Louis Gaudinot was battling it out against an aging wrestler named Nick Cottone, Louis's deficit on the judges' scorecards an indication of Cottone's ability to take him down repeatedly and practically hold him there. Years before, Cottone had tried and failed with this very same tactic against TSK rep Zach at that Reality Fighting event in Wildwood. But this time around it worked, and Cottone was victorious. Meanwhile, at that moment at the Mohegan Sun Arena, Jimmie was winning a decision. Nick was scoring a spectacular Matrix-like flying-knee knockout that would be watched and rewatched over and over again on YouTube. At the ROC at the Tropicana, I was witness to Tiger Schulmann fighters winning by TKO, fighting to a draw, and getting knocked out in thirteen seconds as coach Dave Tirelli shouted instructions from their corners, and hundreds of miles away in Connecticut Uriah had his second MMA bout ever against a veteran with twenty-seven fights under his belt. Uriah won via TKO after putting on a striking clinic. Derek, the reporter, was there at the Mohegan Sun Arena, sitting cageside and texting me the results with commentary, and with each subsequent outcome I saw the members of the Tiger Schulmann family here in Atlantic City react, recipients of their very own updates.

And though I'm an outsider, an observer of this sport and its players, I shared their elation when we all, simultaneously, learned that Lyman had won.

For defeating his opponent at the Bellator welterweight finals, Lyman was crowned their first 170-pound champ, and for the accomplishment of winning his way through the tournament he was handed a check for a whopping $175,000—far more than Lyman had ever made before and the kind of payday reserved for only the UFC's top top-tier guys.

Months passed and I dropped by the Manhattan school. Fedor Emelianenko, a Russian hailed as the greatest heavyweight MMA fighter in the world, was in town as part of a whirlwind media tour, and he was making a stop to shake hands and pose for pictures. When he arrived, he was mobbed like a rockstar. In an office near the entrance to the academy, Ron, Lyman, Uriah, and a few other TSMMA black belts stood with Fedor and grinned for the photo op. Afterward, some of the school's students, lined up and waiting their turn, did the same. In one of the matted classrooms, Uriah—six feet tall and a 200-pound mass of muscle—playfully grappled with a girl no older than eight years old, letting the girl get on his back and sink chokes (he made an almost comedic show of tapping out) or escape when he pinned her down. In another classroom, Nissim took attendance, clipboard in hand.

Lyman joined me in the waiting area.

"Dude, congrats on winning the Bellator tournament," I said. "How does it feel?"

He smiled an easy, genuine smile. That said it all right there.

JAMES

Brooklyn again, this time for a UCL in a boxing gym in Bedford-Stuyvesant, and when I walk in and start dispensing greetings (hellos, thug-hugs, pats on the shoulder), I see James holding court to a circle of enraptured fighters and trainers. In the past week James has earned himself a slice of celebrity of the Internet-hero variety, and I join the circle to hear his version of the tale.

Few things irk MMA fanboys more than charlatans and posers, with sites like Bullshido.net and mixedmartialarts.com chock-full of believers of truth, justice, and the "if you think you can fight then prove it, motherfucker" way, so when someone named Christian claims to be an undefeated prison fighter and opens up a school on Long Island, there's an uproar. The alleged prison fighter catches wind of the uproar and zeroes in on James, whose contributions online aren't anonymous, and it's barely a few hours before the big, bald juicer on the far side of forty is at James's gym, shirtless and making threats.

"I told him, 'Don't hit me for thirty seconds so we can calm down and talk this out,'" James says to us gathered around. "And so he punches me."

There's a takedown, knees to Christian's face until a tooth

flies out, and kicks and punches and stalking on feet until the
police arrive to break up their parking lot soiree. James shows
me grainy cell phone video of the impromptu fight, taken by
his friends present at the time. The promise of seeing the
video has been enough to whip the Internet fanboys into a
frenzy, a frenzy already made wild by Christian coming
online and admitting to the beatdown he'd received at
James's hands. For speaking out against a wannabe and meeting that wannabe head-on, well, therein lies the crux of
James's newfound status. With a dozen sanctioned and
unsanctioned fights under his belt now, he's the real deal in a
sport where the real deal is revered and respected for what
he can actually do, not how well he can talk about doing it.

We in the circle laugh at the circumstances and the details
and the drama—Peter, ignorant of the parking lot fight days
before, has invited Christian to watch this show—and we're
giggling hens and it's funny. But Christian never arrives, and
James, acting as referee for this afternoon's eight-bout smorgasbord of busted eyebrows and blood, is too busy to care.

And for this UCL there most certainly is blood, perhaps
more so because of the rules meeting James conducts before
the show, the hodgepodge of fighters from every shade of
school (or not—a couple don't have schools and admit to just
training themselves) all crowded onto the matted area in a
corner of the gym to hear James tell them that the rules are
vale tudo unless the fighters in a particular bout agree otherwise (ultimately, everyone opts for *vale tudo*, the Unified Rules
be damned). I'm handed an index card listing the match-ups,
each name written out in blue ink, and I recognize more than
a few—Marwin, Chris, Alejandro, Kevin, Lionheart—and
Peter himself is slated to face Rashad. It has all the trappings
of a hearty meal of submission soup and fist salad, and once

the rest of the gang is in place, such as Anil with his camera, Rage with his words of encouragement for his fighters, and the New Generation Karate team with their matching black shirts and sense of purpose, it's on.

Kevin rumbles hard with a rookie called Hybrid, one of Rage's boys, and Hybrid takes a beating until Round 3, when Kevin's forty-eight years of existence catches up to him and he's too exhausted to stop a reversal and the subsequent series of headbutts and punches. Blood, everywhere, and when it's clear Kevin is done James stops it, Hybrid and Rage and the rest of the Brooklyn Fight Factory crew ecstatic and Kevin on all fours with his head down, red pouring down and staining the already well-used and colored canvas. Hybrid poses for the obligatory post-fight pics, Anil directing him where to stand and where to face, and I toss him a "congrats." He leans over and extends his gloved hand. Out of reflex I shake it, and then I'm wiping Kevin's blood off my fingers.

Inexplicably, there's an EMT and a doctor present, a young, white couple with medical bags at the ready, and they take charge of Kevin, leading him to their spot ringside to wash him off and examine him. I watch them work, turn away for a bit, and when I look back the doctor has a needle and some thread in his blue latex-gloved hands, sewing up the torn-open flap of skin above Kevin's eye, the needle in and out, in and out for thirteen stitches total. Kevin sees me and gives me a thumbs-up.

"How did you wind up with those doctors here?" I whisper to Peter when he walks by. He chuckles. "Beats me. They just showed up."

A big, self-trained black guy with a meaningful smile that's present pre-fight, during his fight, and after his fight takes on a bearded white kid named Trevor, Trevor a better kicker and better grappler but outweighed by forty pounds and unable to cope with the black guy's heavy hands. The black guy takes the decision when time runs out, and then it's Peter's turn, and he enters the ring in his usual garb, a judo gi, blue and tied with a red belt, and when he and Rashad go at it the crowd is invested because, though Rashad is still pretty new, everyone present is here because they know Peter in some capacity. Peter swings hard, kicks at his opponent's legs, and ducks in, grabbing at Rashad's shirtless form and struggling to get him down, and like when he fought Joe in Patchogue, Rashad is explosive and athletic, avoiding trouble and throwing punches with mean intentions. But in Round 2, Peter puts Rashad on his back and falls with the Brooklyn Fight Factor rep's foot tucked into his armpit. One twist and Rashad winces and taps out, the victim of a heelhook, and the place erupts in cheers.

Adam the Brooklynite enters the ring and waits in his corner, and the emcee shouts for his opponent to join him. But no one does, and after a few minutes Peter's lackey at the door comes over and says in a low voice, "He cut out. I don't know if he's coming back." We laugh a little at that. It's not the first time a fighter has bailed mid-show, and watching Kevin beaten in such brutal fashion no doubt spurred the exit, so it is humorous, humorous enough that James, the ref in T-shirt, sneakers, and jeans, and even Adam, grin and snigger and shake their heads and smirk.

Chris climbs into the ring and squares off against Alejandro, Alejandro one of Peter's students and still whip-thin and built like a greyhound, and after Chris's respectful handshake the two engage in the kind of chess match that would make every Gracie alive or dead proud, a nonstop, frenetic battle of

submission attempts and "Jesus! How did he get out of that?"
escapes. For all of Round 1, Chris is on the defensive, Houdini
in the realm of tight triangle chokes and rear naked chokes
and armbars, Alejandro affixed to his back like a pissed-off
remora that's had it up to here with that damn shark, and in
Round 2 Psycho pays him back by getting on top and delivering punches, one right after the other. It's anyone's fight in
the final round, and Chris makes one mistake and Alejandro
is stuck on him again, which is enough for the judges (three
folks Peter had simply asked, "Hey, you want to be a judge?"
before the show). Alejandro takes the decision, and I'm left
wondering who in Ring of Combat could've fought like that,
and how it's a shame, a damn shame, Lou's banned UCL
competitors from his show because two highly skilled fighters
equals entertainment—and that was pure entertainment.

"I don't care if I lose as long as I fought hard and to the
best of my ability," Chris says to me afterward. There's no
storming off or pounding on lockers this time. He's satisfied
with his performance, as he should be, and when people
come up to him and tell him he had a good fight, he accepts
it gladly with a "thanks." Chris has a cut near his eye, and in
a moment the doctor is sticking a syringe into his brow, a
local anesthetic, and after comes the needle and thread. Chris
lets out an "Owwwww."

In the ring Kenneth, an experienced amateur from the
New Jersey leagues and fighting under the alias of Buck
McWinters, steamrolls over a green kid named Rafi. (When
James calls Kenneth to the ring, he jokes to the audience that
Buck McWinters is representing the people of Ireland; Ken-
neth is a black.)

Marwin fights, his board shorts and beard and head of
thick, wild hair giving him the appearance of some California

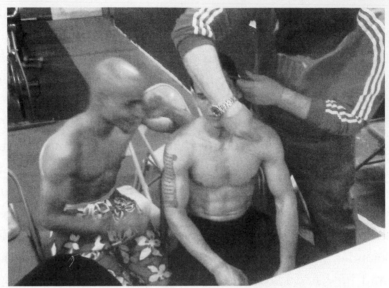

Getting stitches ringside at a UCL in Brooklyn. (*Jim Genia*)

stoner kid, but he's a machine, and with a Team Renzo instructor named Magno cheering him on, Marwin is textbook jiu-jitsu fighter. His opponent, belly down on the canvas and grimacing at Marwin's arm tightening like a boa constrictor around his neck, taps out.

Lionheart follows, another fast-paced battle against someone who punches harder and straighter, and he takes a beating. The first round is halted when Lionheart takes a finger in the eye, and after a few minutes to recover, after the doctor tells him he may have a scratched cornea, it continues with Lionheart finding himself on his opponent's back and working for a choke. But it doesn't come, and the third round, amidst his jumping knee attacks and wild hooks, Lionheart eats an uppercut down the middle and collapses. This time, however, it's the victor who needs stitches, and once Lionheart recovers enough to walk around unaided, he sits beside him with a smile on his face, two battered shirtless warriors sharing a post-fight laugh, an inside joke involving men who pound each other senseless for fun.

There's one more, a three-rounder that sees an Ultimate Karate rep go back and forth with a kid from Long Island, and then it's over.

James comes over to my side of the ring. I tell him that, as no one died, he fulfilled the duties of his refereeing job successfully. This is the first time he's ever officiated a bout.

James knocked out Kirkland in a boxing gym in Washington Heights, the gym located in a basement just north of Fort Tryon park and the audience sitting in metal folding chairs yet mostly standing, erupting when the white kid from Long Island's shin unexpectedly comes up and hits the black kid from the Bronx in the head, an almost surgical separation of man and consciousness. But a year goes by with James inactive ("I sent e-mails to Ring of Combat's matchmaker but he won't answer back," he tells me), and unable to find a promotion where he can turn pro, James ends up taking an amateur bout in Pennsylvania at an event called "Philly Biker Brawl." After winning that one by decision, he shells out the money for the requisite pro fighter medical tests and fills out the paperwork, and with Lembo's blessing returns to the warm embrace of New Jersey's sanctioned amateur MMA circuit, specifically an Asylum Fight League event in a ballroom at the Trump Marina. He gets his opponent to tap out in the second round with a guillotine choke. James is a *vale tudo* shark in a decent-sized pond, a pond full of fish of varying levels of experience, but there are plenty of challenges out there, plenty of barracuda and orca and other sea-borne predators just as ready to make the jump to the pros and just as mean and hungry. It's December 2009, and one such challenge manifests itself in the form of Mike Fischetti, his opponent for the next Asylum show.

11

At nineteen years old, Mike has been a member of the Tiger Schulmann organization since he was eight, now a black belt instructor at their Staten Island school and so homegrown the word *homegrown* itself barely even comes close to describing it. "I've been training with Tiger Schulmann my whole life, so I've been doing everything mixed martial arts from the get-go," he tells me. It's a little over a week before his scheduled fight with James. When he speaks there's youth there, a vibrancy and eagerness pervading his slight Outer Borough accent.

I ask him what he thinks of MMA, his the target generation and cherished demographic of everything combat nowadays. "I love it," he says. "I think it's great because you really get to show the art of the sport. You could just box and never have to worry about getting taken down, or you could grapple and never have to worry about getting punched, but this really takes everything and any type of angle of the sport and puts it to the test. You got a really good fighter and he's got to know how to stand up and fight and he's got to know how to fight on the ground. For a ground guy, they have to learn the stand-up part of it, they can't just learn the jiu-jitsu of it. That's why I really love the sport. It's an all-around test for everything."

He's had one kickboxing bout and three amateur MMA bouts thus far, has yet to taste defeat, and has won via submission and knockout. I ask him about that, about what kind of fighter he considers himself and where his specialty may lie. "I consider myself an all-around fighter. The one thing really good about Tiger Schulmann's is from the beginning it is always 'work your ground, work your stand-up, work everything.' So I really look at myself as an all-around type of fighter. I love the ground, I love to stand up. I've done it all."

We talk about his training routine, but from my conversations with Lyman I know what it must consist of before I even ask. "I train every morning at headquarters," he says. "We train our grappling, we train our kickboxing, we train our cardio. I usually train at night—I do more cardio, more bag training, a little more rolling, and I do some lifting. Every chance I get when I'm not working. But I'm an instructor at the school, so I kind of get to train and work at the same time."

I press him about what it's like training with Lyman, Uriah, Nick, Jimmie, and the rest, and if their successes add any additional weight on his shoulders, the need to perform and excel often just as heavy as the fear of failure. "It's like a big act to follow," Mike says, "but it's so much more of a push to get to train with those guys and get to actually watch them go out and fight and perform. It drives me so much more, it makes me want to be just like that. I get to train with Lyman and Uriah all the time, and to see how good they are and how much talent they have, it really pushes me to push myself ten times harder than I ever would, you know? Lyman has the Bellator championship belt right now, and it's really exciting to know I do the same training as him. I get up every morning and do the same classes as him. To see him hold such a high title like that is really exciting. Hopefully one day I could follow in those footsteps and make a name for myself like they did."

Ask a million fighters to describe their goals and it's always variations of the same UFC or fight-in-Japan dream, and Mike is no different. "My goal is to try and make it big, try to make a living out of it, try and make it to the top. Fight for the UFC or something of that level."

Then I ask him if he knows James, and if so, what he thinks of him. "I met him at my last fight," he says. "He fought at the last Asylum I did. He's a really nice kid, really down-to-earth kid. I'm just gonna go in and fight my fight, really. Go in and stick to the game plan. If he wants to roll I'm gonna roll, if he wants to stand up I'm gonna stand up and do what I gotta do. As of now, I'm just gonna go in there and fight it as the fight comes."

Within days, I'm posing similar questions to the man on the other side of the equation. I catch James at the tail end of his workday and ask how he ended up fighting in legitimate, sanctioned shows again.

"I had one of my potential, of many, pro fights fall through," he says. "I was so ready to fight so I looked on the Internet forums and saw there was one coming up in four days, so I called them up and told them I wanted to fight." Exactly fourteen days after his bout at Philly Biker Brawl he was in the cage at Asylum—fast turnaround for any fighter. "I won that fight and wanted to fight again because I wasn't hurt, so I figured, let's do it again quick."

Why go from underground *vale tudo* to the world of highly regulated fighting? Says James, "I'm sure there's going to be a step up in competition. I'm not sure who else is going to be in the Underground Combat League fighting right now. It's a mixed bag of who's fighting. There's some real badass dudes in there, and then you have some guys with like two weeks of training fighting. So it's a mixed bag." He pauses, perhaps thinking about it, delving deeper within for his answer. "But more so because I just want to get into Ring of Combat or something bigger. I want to make some money, get my name out and do something with it. You know, as far as try a career with it, move on to a bigger show, and I want some glory with it." He adds, "Between you and me, I definitely would go back and do a *vale tudo* fight and say that my twin brother did it if anybody calls me out on it." We laugh together at the idea of that, though it may or may not be a joke. That makes me laugh even harder.

Then I remind him that he'd once foresworn the New Jersey circuit. "I guess it's just easier to find fights in New Jersey," he says. "I'm sure there are plenty of other shows I could've done in other states besides New Jersey that wouldn't care that I did the underground shows and wouldn't even know about it." But a fight, even an amateur one with restrictive rules, is better than no fights at all, and making the trek to somewhere like Massachusetts or farther would be more trouble than it's worth. "I guess in that respect I can say New Jersey's got some good rules and it's nice fighting amateur that way to get some experience in."

Has the transition from no-rules fighting to "civilized" combat been difficult? "No, it's just different," he says, and he draws a comparison to other sports. "Like, is it hard for me to not punch someone in the face when I'm playing basketball?"

"I don't know, is it?" I ask.

"No, not really. I might think that punching someone in the face would be more fun than playing basketball, but I won't break the rules of basketball to have that little bit of fun."

James has only lost three times, the first two instances occurring at a New Breed Fighters and at a show in Ohio, the last one against Josh at a UCL in the Bronx nearly two years ago, the time between Josh's stunning left hook and now filled with training both hard and concise (hard like a day in the Gulag; precise like an Olympic coach's detailed plan for his athlete). The Long Islander trains daily, sometimes two or three times a day, juggling work at that gym in Patchogue with jiu-jitsu class and time at a hardcore boxing gym in a town where the housing is as inexpensive as the street narcotics. "Oh, I'm one of the only white people there," he says. "And it smells really bad, and when I drive into the parking lot there are signs that say 'We are not responsible if your stuff gets stolen.' That's pretty good. That's how you know it's a good gym, because it looks horrible and disgusting. The trainers just yell at you, they yell at you from across the room and won't stop yelling. But it's got to be good, right?"

I ask him if he knows Mike, and if so, what he thinks of him. "I don't really think too much about the guys I'm going to fight. I don't think he fought anybody particularly good . . . He's a sensei at Tiger Schulmann's and those guys are pretty legit as far as their instructors go."

His thoughts on the Tiger Schulmann organization? "I think they get a lot of flack in the community because Tiger Schulmann's is commercialized, but I think that's awesome. Go ahead and make your money, get a good, nice, winning fight team. They obviously prove it with their results, so good for them, you know?"

When James meets Mike in the cage, their bout will be in the midst of over a dozen match-ups, each one with its own storyline, Fighter X defending the honor of his gym or Fighter Y out for revenge because Fighter Z kicked his buddy's ass. Or there may be no storyline at all, the two competitors in the cage simply one athlete testing himself against another. Is there a storyline to the James and Mike pairing? "I really just see it as me versus him," he says. "Just like any other fight. Other people definitely see it as me versus Tiger Schulmann's, or as the UCL versus New Jersey, definitely as underground fighters versus legit fighters. People I work with see it as a little no-name gym versus the big, commercialized monster in Tiger Schulmann's. And I just see it as, I'm going to punch him in the face and hope for the best."

I ask him to make a prediction, and in typical James fashion he does without hesitation, a hint of humor in his words. "I would like to jiu-jitsu him to death," says the Funaro brother who would've beaten the crap out of Joe if Joe had given up in his fight with Kirkland, the Funaro brother who frequently promises offerings of blood to Crom (yes, the deity Conan the Barbarian patronizes) whenever he's online and who doesn't hesitate when an enraged meathead shows up at his gym. "With a triangle choke," says James. "That would be cool."

III

The Raritan Expo Center is vast, cavernous, and quite literally freezing, and though when I walk in I'm greeted warmly by Carl the promoter, it does nothing to take the edge off the cold. It's two hours before showtime, two hours before the lights go down around the cage and get bright within and the crowd comes alive with hoots and cheers. But now there's emptiness and quiet, interrupted briefly by the DJ adjusting the sound with test tracks, while here and there mill a few fighters, staff, and coaches. Near the concession stand is James, chatting casually with Kenneth and another fighter, and I make a beeline to shake their hands, my stock "How are you?" met with a stock "Great, good, fine," a pre-show ritual as meaningless as a fist-bump between strangers yet as meaningful as a "good luck" between friends. Not too long ago were the official weigh-ins, and Kenneth is lamenting the cut and how difficult it was, this one his lowest venture thus far, 142 pounds to face a Tiger Schulmann 141-pounder; James stepped on the scale 173 to his opponent's 174. Then they're off, backstage or wherever, to put themselves further into the zone and mentally prepare for what they'll soon subject themselves to.

Sachs, the Tiger Schulmann organization's chief financial officer and a key behind-the-scenes player in all things New Jersey mixed martial arts, enters and is swarmed by TSMMA soldiers clad in black, Mike among them, the nineteen-year-old sporting short dark hair with an array of designs buzzed in. I wade into the circle and Sachs and I exchange pleasantries, and after I shake Fischetti's hand and ask him how he's feeling, the young bucks disappear, too, leaving Sachs and me to talk shop. By now there have been twenty-three Asylum events, this one the twenty-fourth, and I've been to three. My presence here is solely to watch James and Mike go at it, and with that knowledge and a smile, Sachs has labeled James as my "guy," as if I were training or managing him or had some sort of vested interest in the outcome.

Never having seen Mike fight before and knowing I'll get an honest and truthful answer, I ask Sachs what to expect from him. Sachs admits that jiu-jitsu may be his weakest area, but that when it comes to stand-up, Mike is deadly. Absolutely deadly. We gossip a bit—as the Tiger Schulmann back office handles the administrative stuff for Asylum and Ring of Combat, Sachs is in someway tied into it all—and then I claim a seat at one of the tables ringing the outside of the cage and wander. Backstage is K-Rod, smiling and quick with a hug, one of his teammates fighting late in the card for a belt. Lembo breezes by with paperwork in hand. In one of the big, carpeted conference rooms the fighters and their teams have set up, each group lining the wall and a scant five or ten feet from the other, each group its own little clique and own little world. As I stand in the room's open center taking in the scene, Dave Tirelli breaks away from the TSMMA contingent and greets me. "I wish I could get back in there," he says, the grizzled elder statesman clearly longing for what his fighting days made him feel. But the wheel has turned, and nowadays Dave is working part-time for the New Jersey commission, in training as a fight judge and aiming toward an eventual refereeing gig. He, too, informs me that Mike is a killer and so young and so talented, his words not unlike a proud papa's, and I notice Elvis sitting there and reach down to shake his hand, cracking wise that I have to be gentle lest it break. Elvis laughs.

In the hall outside the conference room sits another group of fighters, James among them, and when I make my way to the cage the place has begun to fill up, the rows and rows of folding chairs claimed as temporary property by the friends and family and anyone tangentially connected to the fighters and those just fans of action. Joe is there, in the front row, and one of James's coaches, who is confident that James will have his way with his opponent. (What coach or teammate would ever say his fighter is doomed? I have yet to encounter one.) The clock ticks, each successive minute bringing more spectators and ratcheting up the tension, until it's time, time for the start and time for the fighting.

Two giant inflatable musclemen stand sentry at the portal from backstage, and on a TV screen above the metal-framed entranceway the Asylum Fight League name flickers in red and white letters, the orchestrated and centralized fanfare a landmark in the fighters' walk to the cage and a rallying point where all can watch each entourage in those few moments before battle. First through it are a pair of relative newcomers, and after their bout ends with an armbar, Kenneth and his taller, lankier Tiger Schulmann representative make the journey, Kenneth trailed by his corner man and clad in bold pink shorts bearing the insignia of Katz's school. This one goes the distance, Kenneth too fast with his kicks and possessing more than enough athleticism and balance to keep it on the feet whenever his foe tries to get it to the ground, and when time runs out he takes the decision.

Another bout, then another, and Lou arrives to take a seat beside me. "His guy is fighting one of our guys," Sachs informs him. My protestations bring hearty chuckles.

"James Funaro and Mike Fischetti will be the fight of the year," says Carl, and at that it seems Lou's interest is piqued. Meanwhile, in the cage a 170-pound Long Islander knocks out a Brazilian, a Longo-trained fighter wins a decision, and then the bout we at the table are waiting for.

Shirtless, focused, his short brown hair edged with sweat from his warm-up, James takes the walk—the walk—to "Rock You Like a Hurricane" by the Scorpions, and he pauses for a commission inspector wearing latex gloves to give him a once-over (a little Vaseline on the ridges of the face is fine; too much is a no-no) before climbing up and into what will be the field of war. Eminem blares and out comes Mike, shrouded in black sweatshirt and just as focused, and the crowd, partisan for this instructor from Staten Island, makes it very clear who they want to win. Once inside the chain-link crucible, Mike raises his gloved fist up, a gladiator saluting his fans. "Your guy asked for this match-up," says Sachs, as if James was picking a fight in the "I'm going to kick your ass" sense, but when Mike does a circuit and passes his opponent, he and James show each other nothing but respect, all business like it's just a job. My chair is almost directly behind the imaginary corner where Mike must stand ready, and he looks down at me and nods, nods his acknowledgment at Tiger and Ron Schulmann sitting in the first row nearby. The referee, an experienced fighter named Tom who years ago fought underground in New York, stands between the two and there's silence, a dramatic instant of calm, then "Go!"

James and Mike approach the center of the cage, stalking, pensive, analytical, but a blur of hands and they're trading, Mike's straighter punches finding their mark on James's face and making the Long Islander's fists go wild. James ducks and shoots, wrapping his arms around the TSMMA rep's front leg for a takedown that's met with a shift of the hips and an explosive change of direction. More leather, flying like lead in a gunfight, and James is struggling to get Mike down, going so far as to jump up and wrap his legs around him in an effort to pull him to the canvas. That move is successful, yet when James swivels for an armbar his prey deftly steps away. Tom comes between them and gestures for Mike to take a neutral corner, signals for the doctor; standing upright with his hands on his hips, James is taking in deep breaths. From his nose, and from a few small cuts, trickles blood. The crowd, by now berserk, explodes with ugly glee.

Still, it's not over, and when the doctor wipes the wounded fighter down and gives the ref the thumbs-up, it resumes, this time with an air of desperation pervading James's actions. He attempts a flashy roll to rope Mike in, crouches low and reaches for a stray knee or ankle, and when that bears no fruit he squares up and strikes, firing off a kick and then punches—again, his fists losing their trajectory when Mike hits him first. Two minutes and twenty-seven seconds have elapsed in the bout and James's nose is gushing, a splatter pattern painting him and Mike both. Now Tom has seen enough and he waves it off. Mike has won.

You hear a million times how winning a fight is the best feeling in the world, and when Mike nimbly hops up and straddles the cage, a nineteen-year-old well-tuned machine tested in combat, the best way to describe the expression on his face as he soaks in the cheers is ecstasy. Pure ecstasy.

James has a towel to his brow where the worst of his cuts lie, and when Mike comes down and meets him again in the center they embrace, the Tiger Schulmann rep even raising James's arm up, the universal post-fight show of appreciation and an unspoken plea to the crowd to give this man just humbled and defeated some love, too. They do, they all do, and it reaches a climax when the announcer makes the win via TKO official. Mike exits the cage a hero, striding forward into a sea of fans and supporters.

It takes the Asylum staff ten minutes to mop up James's blood from the canvas.

Backstage again, and I enter the big conference room where Mike sits surrounded by teammates. His arm is extended, and one of his corner men is using a pair of medical scissors to cut off his hand wraps. I congratulate him and he thanks me.

"What was your game plan?" I ask him.

"To keep punching him and not let him take me down," he replies. His grin is from ear to ear and threatening to take over his whole face.

I roam a bit more and find James. He's in his regular

clothes now, and from a nostril juts a blood-soaked piece of tissue, an apt accoutrement to the thick Band-Aids covering the two massive cuts above and around his left eye. There are abrasions, too, on his lip and cheeks and forehead, and his eye socket is getting darker with each passing second. "You'll be back," I tell him, but when he speaks—promising to come back harder, promising to get the rematch, promising to not make the same mistakes again—his voice and the quiver of his bottom lip betray the kind of emotion that renders whatever I may say complete and utter bullshit. To win may be the highest of highs, but to lose, especially after devoting so much time and effort and sweat and pain and blood to something you wanted so bad, well, that right there is the essence of "suck," distilled and refined into a shot glass that few will ever have the displeasure of sipping.

But win or lose, James is a fighter in every sense of the word. When he fell to Josh in the UCL, a number of James's friends were there to witness it, there to cheer him on had he won and struck silent in shock when he lost. He came back stronger than ever then. "It happens, James," I say, this time patting him on the shoulder for emphasis. "But you'll be back."

"Thanks for coming down to watch," he says, an unspoken apology hanging there like when his brother lost to Rashad, as if only his victory would've made the frigid night in Raritan worth it. It was worth it, though, it always is regardless of who falters or comes out on top, the privilege of watching two warriors strive and try to give their all for the ultimate payoff. It's not about who wins and who loses. It's about the journey to the cage, the conflict and confrontation, and that time afterward when all violence is pushed aside, replaced by a code thousands of years old and under-

stood by only a chosen few. And from my seat cageside, I get
to witness it all.

"No," I say to him. "It was my pleasure. Thank you."

IV

I ask Peter what he thinks of James losing at the Asylum Fight
League event. One thing Peter is not short on is opinion, and
he's quick to give his.

"I think it fucking sucks," he says. "But that's what he
gets for entering those amateur competitions. I mean, he
couldn't take the guy down, and if he did he wouldn't have
been able to maul the guy because of the rules. Either way,
he was kind of destined to lose that fight because of the
rules."

Within a day, James was already joking about his loss, and
he posted a picture of his battered face online. A few days
after that he was back training, promising more blood—his
own or his future opponent's—to Crom. But there was still
some unfinished business in the form of Christian the alleged
prison fighter, who'd acquired a taste for the online notoriety
his initial parking lot fisticuff had garnered him. He wanted
another crack at the Funaro brother, wanted whatever attention and interviews and blogspace he could squeeze out of
his faux-feud with James.

At first, Peter made the match-up for one of his events,
but it never materialized, Christian no-showed and followed
it up with texts depicting fantasies of drug binges, rehab,
arrests, car accidents—the works. Yet on a night in March,
four months after the Mike Fischetti bout in New Jersey, it
came together, an 11:00 P.M. soiree at James's gym in
Patchogue. I didn't go but Anil was there, snapping away

with his camera at Christian arriving, emerging from the darkness of the parking lot out behind the building and in through the back door, upstairs and in the ring, Christian gaunt and covered in tattoos, James stalking him and putting him down quickly and effortlessly with rights and lefts. And moments later, when Christian was on his back, slowly returning to consciousness, James was sitting cross-legged beside him, gloves off and holding one of Christian's hands as he came to.

It was by no means a "big" fight—Randy Couture was defeating Mark Coleman in Las Vegas in the Octagon then, and all over the world regional champions were staking their claim and climbing their respective ladders—but to a community that existed in New York and in forums online, James's once-and-for-all handling of Christian was sweet and satisfying. The underground veteran may have met with defeat at the hands of one of Tiger Schulmann's most promising up-and-comers, but he was still a well-honed weapon. It was still undeniable that James could fight for real.

KIMBO

Kimbo Slice, the most accomplished underground fighter of all time (from Miami; they just do it in backyards there), made his way to the cage, an entourage of friends, supporters, and hangers-on trailing behind him as the cameras flashed and the crowd, 8,033 strong and hungry for blood, cheered. With his muscles and pure, unadulterated meanness, Kimbo (real name, Kevin Ferguson) was a massive action figure of carved ebony, like something a Roman centurion would've brought back from conquests in far-off lands. The word *intimidating* didn't even come close, didn't do him the least bit of justice. He was frightening, everything you'd expect from someone well-known for kicking ass and moments from kicking some ass again. Standing at the door to the cage, he looked ready.

Welcome to May 2008, and EliteXC's first joint venture with CBS, a night of knockouts, hematomas, injured eyes, and exploding ears. A night of MMA action dubbed *Primetime*, and the sport's first-ever venture into live primetime television and mainstream acceptance. Welcome to history.

Bald-headed, monstrous fists barely contained by the four-ounce fingerless gloves, Kimbo was a 235-pound nightmare of pugilistic fury. The undercard of tonight's event at the Prudential Center in Newark had provided fans in attendance with all sorts of variations on the theme "two men enter, one man leaves," but over seven million have tuned in to watch the Internet legend throw down, a legend and bare-knuckle boxer and the baddest of the bad, known for blasting opponents with left hooks and right crosses on YouTube. Seven million watching and waiting for a glimpse at brutality.

The announcer spoke into the microphone, rambling on about EliteXC, CBS, the New Jersey State Athletic Control Board, and then mentioning the players in this impending chess match of blood. Opponent James Thompson, a towering Brit weighing 257 pounds and standing almost six and a half feet tall, barely got a response from the crowd. The mere utterance of the name Kimbo Slice threatened to bring the Prudential Center's walls down. At cageside, commentators Gus Johnson, Mauro Ranallo, and Frank Shamrock talked of Kimbo's heavy hands, of Thompson's aggressive style and glass jaw and propensity for charging right in at the opening bell, and getting knocked out half the time. Referee Big Dan called the combatants to the center for their staredown. Kimbo, the shorter of the two by a couple of inches, glared up at Thompson with all sorts of hatred. The Brit glared back with a dozen different kinds of loathing, and Big Dan, caught in the middle, was in danger of bursting into flame, spontaneously combusting from the intensity. Somewhere, a grandmother watching at home fainted in her living room. Somewhere, a family dog yelped and hid under a table.

"Kimbo's grappling skills are suspect, so Thompson's only chance is to get the fight to the ground," stated the various armchair quarterbacks sitting in media row, spewing the obvious like lines meant to impress girls in bars. "But Thompson's no grappler, so this bout is a gift," they said. "Yeah, a gift," they said, and I stared too hard at the screen of my laptop, desperate to avoid their vortex of inanity.

Kimbo and Thompson moved back to their opposing sides of the cage. In his time fighting in Japan, before crowds numbering between ten to forty thousand, Thompson's method of fighting had been nicknamed the "Gong and Dash" (think: a gong is sounded and he dashes across the ring). In his time prior to entering mixed martial arts, well before he notched twenty-two professional bouts under his belt, Thompson's job had been to kick Gypsy squatters off land owners' properties. The violence he had doled out then paled in comparison to the violence about to be witnessed now.

Involve television and these things must run on tight, mapped-out schedules, so Big Dan watched for the signal from the television producer outside the cage, and when he got it he yelled to the combatants asking if they were ready. It wasn't hard to imagine jets of steam coming from Thompson's ears. It wasn't hard to imagine Kimbo's engine rev higher and higher. Then the referee yelled for them to fight.

And Thompson, going against every expectation, avoided the Gong and Dash and Kimbo's fists full of dynamite, and despite the best efforts of the massive Miami native with legions upon legions of fans, the behemoth Brit managed to take him down.

The most watched bout ever in U.S. history was underway.

EliteXC's Primetime was a long way from when the Ultimate Fighting Championship first debuted on pay-per-view in 1993, a long way from the *vale tudo* matches in Brazil in the 1920s, and one heck of a long way from the interschool, interdiscipline bouts in Japan's post-feudal era. But no other sport

had the variety, ferocity, and authenticity of mixed martial
arts, no other sport had athletes as physically conditioned or
psychologically complex, and no other sport captured the
imagination quite like this one. Consequently, CBS wanted in
on the party.

Kimbo struggled underneath Thompson's massive form.
He was on his back and pressed up against the edge of the
cage now, and the Brit was grounding and pounding, raining
down elbows and forearms like an angry Norse god shower-
ing lightning bolts on rampaging giants. But an adrenaline
dump and utter exhaustion had made those lightning bolts
more like a collection of sparks, more show than heat, but that
was beside the point. Kimbo was in trouble. As per the rules
of this heavily regulated match, a fighter could tap out, and if
he couldn't intelligently defend himself, the referee had the
power to stop the bout and declare the attacker the winner.
Stuck beneath the heavier Thompson, Kimbo didn't look like
he was going anywhere.

"Work out of there or I'm gonna stop it," Big Dan bel-
lowed, and at those words Thompson increased his output,
his face a Kabuki mask of raw aggression. The number of
unanswered blows Kimbo absorbed approached seventy and
there was still plenty of time left in Round Two.

Don't let their mean mugs and pre-fight bravado fool you,
because for all the snarls and posturing, these two fighters are
pleasant and likeable people in real life. At the press conference before Kimbo's first MMA fight in July 2005, an exhibition bout against former boxing heavyweight world
champion Ray Mercer, the backyard brawler took the microphone and promised all sorts of doom and punishment. But
he was respectful about it. In mixed martial arts, no one
threatens to eat an opponent's kids or has to worry about get-

ting their ear bitten off, and even the trash talk is tempered with civility. Get to know just a handful of fighters and the nature of the beast reveals itself as a dichotomy, rabid in combat, purring outside of it.

Rewind to the EliteXC Primetime presser, held in a trendy, multilevel midtown Manhattan nightclub in the afternoon. Things weren't quite underway yet and the stage, chairs, and podium set up in a corner were empty. Instead, the fighters on the undercard mingled with their corner men, their trainers, and members of the media, while the healthiest food spread ever, consisting of fruits and vegetables, was splayed out on a table. Some journo had a microphone in Matt Hughes's face, and when I ran into Peter and Lembo, I introduced them to each other, the Sith Lord of the Underground and the Jedi Master of Sanctioning shaking hands without meaning it. Kimbo sat apart, his entourage telling everyone who approached that he wasn't ready to speak, and Thompson, his biceps perilously close to splitting the short sleeves of his white T-shirt, smiled as he stared into a Channel 2 News camera. The reporter had just asked him how he felt about being brought in to lose.

The reporter was spot-on. EliteXC was a six-month-old organization headed by boxing promoter Gary Shaw, and while industry giant Zuffa, LLC (owner of the Ultimate Fighting Championship) was making money hand over foot, this upstart promotion was still struggling to gain a foothold. It was somewhat of a coup that Shaw's baby had leapfrogged the UFC and made it to network television first, but with most top fighters under contract with the enemy, the problem of creating a fight card the public wanted to see remained. Kimbo, the underground Internet superstar and YouTube sensation, was far and away the biggest draw Shaw had. Heaven forbid if Kimbo got his butt kicked on national television. What would EliteXC do then?

Thompson did not squash the reporter for asking the question, nor betray any anger or ignorance or denial. His last fight with the organization ended with him unconscious after two minutes and twenty-four seconds, and the man who beat him—a malevolent black Minnesotan with a Mohawk, whom many thought should have been facing Kimbo instead—was relegated to the under card. Thompson knew the score. He smiled, laid on the compliments and respect for Kimbo, and said he had a plan. He wasn't lying.

In wrestling it's all about the pin. In boxing, it's the KO, TKO, or judges' decision. In MMA, it's all over when a fighter scores a knockout with a kick, punch, knee to the grill, elbow to the dome, or even a hard throw or takedown that snatches the victim's consciousness right out from under him. The bout can end via submission—a potentially bone-breaking armlock or leglock, or a choke that can (and sometimes does) put an opponent out cold, moves that are warded off with a tap out signaling, "Okay, okay, you caught me." Add to that the aforementioned TKO and the judges' decision if the bout goes the distance, and you have yourself a bout under the Unified Rules.

The crowd at the pristine Prudential Center, a venue that normally housed the New Jersey Devils hockey team but was instead hosting the biggest MMA event outside of the UFC, shouted their approval when Big Dan brought the two combatants to their feet. He had the discretion to do so when he felt the action had stalled, and as neither fighter had been working to improve their position, stalled the bout was. Yet the stand-up only fueled the grumbling from media row, grumbles and murmurs and complaints about the seventy-one unanswered blows that most felt should've ended the fight in the Brit's favor right then and there. A *Sports Illustrated* reporter named Josh shook his head. An Internet radio personality named Eddie muttered words like *sham* and *fix*. The bell rang, indicating the end of the second round, and the two exhausted warriors made their way to their corners ("corners" a figurative word, as technically there are none in a circular cage).

No one had expected the battle to go this long, nor had they expected Thompson to actually execute a thought-out game plan. The only flaw in his strategy had been that, though he had managed to get Kimbo to the ground with dogged takedowns (techniques learned courtesy of his time training with UFC champion Randy Couture), Thompson lacked the finer grappling skills required to snag a submission. It's one thing to get someone down; it's another thing entirely to get an arm around their neck and choke them out.

The sixty-second rest period barely gave them time to catch their breath, their respective coaches and corners working feverishly like NASCAR pit crews, squirting water into mouths and dabbing at sweaty brows with a towel and spewing instructions or encouragement, and then the referee signaled that the last round was underway. If it were to go to the judges' scorecards now, there would be no question the first two rounds belonged to Thompson, so Kimbo's last great hope was to swing for the fences and pray something connected. Sure, when the Nielsen ratings would be released in a few days and the breakdowns pointed to the event, and this bout especially, as a runaway ratings success—far outstripping the UFC's biggest fights to date—Shaw and the EliteXC staff could break out the champagne and make toasts. But right here, right now in the cage, Kimbo had less than five minutes to salvage his "unbeatable street fighter" mystique.

He did it in thirty-eight seconds. A right hook to the side of Thompson's head and the Brit's ear, already swollen and cauliflower-like from hard training, burst in an explosion of gore. He stumbled, and Kimbo followed up with hooks, uppercuts, mean faces, and a strong desire to get the fight—his longest one ever—over with. Thompson didn't go down but he looked out of it. Big Dan stepped in and waved the bout off, and Kimbo collapsed to the canvas, his arms raised in victory as he huffed and puffed and stared up at the lights. Still on his feet, a bewildered Thompson pushed Big Dan in frustration. A chorus of boos echoed from the audience. The commentators at cageside questioned the stoppage, and those sitting in press row formulated conspiracy theories involving the referee, the athletic commission, Shaw, EliteXC, shooters on the grassy knoll, and Sasquatch.

But none of that mattered. Tomorrow, more media outlets would talk about the sport than ever before. People would talk about Kimbo's performance on the trading floors of investment banks and in Starbucks, and they would describe Thompson's ruptured ear on subways and in restaurants. They would talk about the UFC, and about who really was the best fighter in the world. And they would talk about the biggest night in the sport's history. But most of all, thanks to two very scary men, a cage, and an exploding ear in the most-watched U.S. MMA bout ever, they would talk about Kimbo.

11

There's an economical hierarchy ingrained into the fiscal side of mixed martial arts, a rigid and inflexible set of laws that end up leeching out the bank accounts of investors and send

organizational executives to bankruptcy court, briefcases full
of receipts and explanations in hand. First and foremost, if
you're a fighter, the UFC is where the money lies. Sure, maybe
you're a big enough ticket seller or attraction to warrant a
regional promotion's shelling out of the bucks, but odds are
you're not, and either way, few, if any, regional gigs can pay
like the UFC can, especially when factors like sponsorships,
merchandising rights, and pay-per-view percentages get
added to the equation. No East Coast, West Coast, Midwest,
Canada-based, or overseas event gets the national (and international) exposure to command anything close to that level
of advertising money, and in terms of sheer revenue numbers . . . well, let's just say an accountant working for the UFC
garners a lot more love and attention than an accountant
working for another MMA promotion at those accounting
convention socials.

Then there's the concept of making stars. Dominate in a
Ring of Combat and maybe people will drive from New York
and Pennsylvania to see you fight, but not always, and aside
from an occasional spot on HDNet Fights or a glimpse of
your handiwork on late-night TV, your star can only shine so
bright. The UFC, though, with its seemingly perpetual contract with SpikeTV, its pay-per-view broadcasts and multime-
dia muscle, makes stars—and with that star-making power
comes the ability to dictate pay, and through contracts, the
control of who gets released in time to work for a competitor
and who doesn't. For his first bout in the UFC's Octagon,
former UCL fighter Frankie made six thousand dollars (his
$3,000 "show" money, which is his for just being there, plus
his $3,000 "win" money), and because his performance was
nonstop thrills and action, he was awarded a discretionary
and coveted "Fight of the Night" bonus in the sum of twenty

grand—far more than Frankie has ever made as a top dog in New Jersey. That, coupled with the multi-bout contract he'd signed, and it was clear the Toms River native would be calling the UFC his home for a while. And if he kept racking up the wins, creating a sizeable enough fan base to drive pay-per-view sales, then why wouldn't the UFC give him the promotional push needed to make him a star? His contract would prevent other shows from luring him away, and with that kind of green coming in Frankie would have no reason to want to fight anywhere else. (Months before his Octagon debut, I ran into Frankie in the locker room before a show. He was there to corner teammates, and when I asked him what he had on his plate, what loomed on the horizon for one of the Garden State's best, he answered in his usual verbosity: "Got to get paid, man.")

These are the laws of the economics of mixed martial arts, as immutable as the U.S. Constitution, as holy as the tablets Moses lugged down Mount Sinai, as true as Heavenly Gospel. And Kimbo, from the very outset of his career, broke them.

Born in 1974 in the Bahamas and raised in South Florida, Kimbo rose from the obscurity of an athletic scholarship and a bid to play for the Miami Dolphins to work as a driver and bodyguard for friend Icey Mike, the man behind Reality-Kings, a production company that specialized in web porn but which eventually put the hulking slugger on camera for organized backyard brawls. It wasn't quite MMA, but it struck a similar chord, that "Holy crap, these are some badass underground fights!" that made the UCL a viable product. A fan base grew, and for defeating the likes of Big Mac, Afro Puff, and "the Bouncer," he was earning three to five grand a fight simply for being one of the scariest dudes on the planet. In 2004, Icey Mike issued a challenge on mixedmartialarts.com, calling for someone, anyone, to step up and face Kimbo's fury in an underground boxing match. A Boston police officer and Golden Gloves champ accepted the challenge, and the two waged a ten-minute war that Kimbo eventually lost. Yet the hype machine never stopped humming. After that 2004 fight, recorded at some secret location (a gym? A homeless shelter? Someone's basement? It doesn't get any more underground than that, folks), the UFC put the Boston cop into the Octagon, where he promptly lost and was never brought back. It was clear Kimbo was the one they had wanted, the one they should have gotten, and I heard rumors that the UFC brass made him a low-ball offer that he had no problem balking at, especially with minor league organizations offering him far, far more than what the UFC's typical payscale would've allowed. Kimbo was a pre-packaged star and a draw at the highest levels, despite having merely a fraction of the experience and skill of other heavyweights. Why bother fighting for peanuts when in one fell swoop he could be the cornerstone of an upstart promotion and feed his six kids in style?

Boardwalk Hall, June 2007. The fifth installment of the Cage Fury Fighting Championship, with 7,300 people packed into an old, cavernous venue that once hosted the Beatles and the 1964 Democratic National Convention but now barely contained the excitement and electricity that surrounded Kimbo's first MMA bout. From cageside I listened to his opponent, former WBO heavyweight boxing champ Ray Mercer, receive barely a modicum of crowd response when he made his entrance, but when Kimbo appeared it was as if the Earth was shaking to its very core. Messiahs don't get this kind of love. On the under card, Lyman took out Doug while a sea of Team Tiger Schulmann supporters screamed, and

Gregor Gracie's win via choke merited its own vociferous approval, but right now everyone in attendance was on their feet, bringing their hands together for a six foot two, 249-pound superstar getting paid upwards of seventy-five thousand bucks for what would end up being one minute and twelve seconds of heart-pounding pandemonium.

You can gauge a bout's importance by the density of the press row, and this one was thick with know-nothing boxing writers attracted to the scent Mercer was putting off, writers no doubt talented but who, when Gregor wrapped his arms around his opponent and put his hands in place for a bent-armlock, saw only two men hugging. I sat amongst them, sometimes answering their questions, and then took a seat beside the cage for the main event. As Kimbo versus Mercer could only be sanctioned as an exhibition and New Jersey State Athletic Control Board-employed officials can't sit for exhibition bouts, Lembo had asked me to be a judge. Yet no one harbored even a remote belief that this one would go to a decision, and a guillotine choke by Kimbo—the most rudimentary but effective of submission moves, used to put pressure on the necks of foes charging in with their heads down—had proved us all right. From cageside I listened to the deafening crescendo of cheers and watched the celebration, and Kimbo was ushered by Icey Mike and his entourage backstage and sequestered in his locker room. A YouTube star was now a bonafide MMA star.

"I'm zero and one in mixed martial arts and I'm going to stay zero and one in mixed martial arts," said Mercer afterward to us media gathered around. "I never thought I was going to get choked—especially with the 'bad-ass streetfighter' reputation he had." Mercer was disappointed things didn't go his way, no doubt a bit sore that a bare-knuckle boxer was showered with more affection than a returning Roman conqueror while he was a mere redheaded stepchild. Like a pugilistic refugee, he would flee the cage, only returning years later to knock out a fallen-from-grace UFC champ at a B-level show in Alabama. Kimbo, meanwhile, would go on to bigger things. A fleeting investor and tumbling financial house of cards would make this event the Cage Fury Fighting Championship's last, but for Kimbo, it was just the beginning.

III

The legend goes that EliteXC was formed when Shaw was visited by angels and struck by visions of grandiose fighting affairs featuring an Animatronic dragon and larger-than-life production values, and that to realize these visions, he gathered around him executives who ran some of the most successful regional shows in the country—a cabal of sorts, of the industry's brightest and most experienced.

Then he ignored them.

EliteXC wasted little time in scooping up Kimbo after the Cage Fury Fighting Championship went under, and the bout that was to headline the sixth Cage Fury Fighting Championship, a face-punching party between Kimbo and washed-up UFC veteran Tank Abbott, was pushed to February 2007. Before then, EliteXC pitted their new star against a minor league tomato can at a show in Texas, and after Kimbo's nineteen-second crushing of said can, the UFC suddenly had a legitimate competitor (albeit one hemorrhaging money and mismanaged at the very top). For, although the organization had put out seven shows before Kimbo came on board, he was just the thing needed to go from broadcasts on Showtime to the realm of CBS primetime and worldwide recognition, and his forty-three-second knockout of Tank at the BankUnited Center in Florida only further entrenched his role as the cornerstone of the company's success. And eventually, the nucleus of its failure.

Failure is a very real, very probable thing that looms over promotions aiming for a cut of consumer dollars; it looms like the shadow of a monster, standing just over the shoulder exhaling hot breath on the back of the neck. The month before EliteXC's Primetime, I was at the Izod Center in East Rutherford, ringside for what would be the International Fight League's second-to-last show ever, and failure sat in every vacant seat in the arena, scoffing at the top-notch regional-level fights, laughing at every excess dollar spent on multi-colored jerseys for contrived team names, and smirking at the unnecessary bells and whistles for a live show no one would see nor care about. The IFL was one of many upstart organizations that thought it could wrest a piece of pie from the UFC's hands, yet despite the wealth and business acumen of its principal players, real estate developer Kurt Otto and *Wizard* magazine publisher Gareb Shamus, from the start it was a place where fighters could get overpaid before the well ran dry. Rumor had it that the promoter for the Cage Fury Fighting Championship was asked by one of his investors to see the books, to see what money was coming in and what was going out, and that's when it all hit the fan, but the IFL was a public company; anyone could find their quarterly statements online and see just how quickly the ship was sinking. (In January 2007, a share of the IFL was worth seventeen bucks; in June 2008, a share was worth a nickel.) "Captain, there's an iceberg with the word *failure* written in big letters on it in our path," said the sailor, and Otto and Shamus screamed, "Full steam ahead!"—the two seemingly very eager to bring their vessel to the bottom of the sea to join the wrecks of the Cage Fury Fighting Championships, the World Fighting Alliance, Pride Fighting Championships, and others.

EliteXC's perilous proximity to that iceberg was common knowledge after the Thompson fight. Gone now was Shaw, relegated to an advisory role while others—like Turi, one of the aforementioned brightest and experienced—did the legwork needed to churn out respectable MMA events and keep the organization from going under. But the company was almost out of cash thanks to overspending and bad decisions, and someone would need to foot the bill for them to put on another show.

Kimbo's bout with Thompson snagged 7,281,000 viewers, making it an impossible-to-ignore ratings hit, and when Elite-XC's follow-up to Primetime, *Unfinished Business*, did dismal ratings without Kimbo on the card, the stage was set for *Heat*, a CBS-funded event that featured Kimbo's return to live network television with a match-up against aged legend Ken Shamrock. At stake was more than Kimbo's spotless record, more than a variety of fighters' careers and livelihoods, and more than simply another option for fans desirous for something that does not take place in the Octagon. No, with representatives from CBS cageside for Heat, poised with pens over contracts, ready to buy the struggling but well-known, well-branded organization, there was a lot more at stake than that.

IV

I arrived at the Bank Atlantic Center just outside of Fort Lauderdale at 5:00 P.M. for the October EliteXC Heat event, my col-

leagues and I gathered like war correspondents waiting for
the next Huey to Danang or Blackhawk to Camp Rhino.
Radio reporter Randy Harris was there, as was *American
Shaolin* author Matt Polly, writer Derek, and photographer
Zack, all of us anxious and hopeful and anticipating a night of
match-ups either intriguing or comical, when, after we picked
up our laminated credentials, the security guard let it slip. "I
heard over my radio that the main event is off," he said.
"Someone named Shamrock is injured. He ain't fighting."
Harris was incredulous, but his phone calls to Shamrock went
unanswered, while in the press room the EliteXC equivalent
of White House press secretary feigned indifference with the
same degree of believability as that of a deer caught in the
middle of a street, feigning indifference in the headlights of an
oncoming tractor trailer. Any MMA historian worth his salt
would have drawn comparisons to UFC 24, when headliner
Kevin Randleman had slipped on pipes backstage thereby
sinking that event, or when Matt Serra's debut in Pride FC
had been scrapped when his opponent was set afire during a
pyrotechnic-heavy entrance. But this mess about to unfold on
network television was in a league of its own.

No one on the company payroll would confirm or deny
the rumor of Shamrock's injury, but soon the swelling ranks
of journalists disappearing backstage into the locker rooms
and reappearing like Viet Cong with base layouts and other
vital information was enough for at least a rough sketch of
the situation: Shamrock, sparring too hard at the last minute,
had received a laceration above his eye that required stitches,
and the Florida State Boxing Commission was in no way,
shape, or form allowing him to compete. Was it truly an acci-
dent or did he do it to himself? The MMA legend had had no
problems giving Kimbo a shove to play the role of heel at the

weigh-ins the day before, but at 206 pounds to his opponent's
defined 234, it was clear that, at best, Shamrock was going to
phone his performance in, and at worst . . . Well, think of the
lengths a man, jealous of the size of an Internet star's paycheck, would go to screw his employers. You get the idea.
Besides, as anyone in the industry could tell you, a cut of that
nature would be sealed up with Krazy Glue faster than you
could say, "No sir, Doctor, I have absolutely nothing to say
during this pre-fight physical. Nope. Nothing at all." Rumors
abounded, swirling like a tornado of whispered half truths
and guesses, each one accompanied by a shake of the head or
a roll of the eyes. Was the heavyweight Kimbo really being
offered one of the 205-pound light heavyweights meant for
the undercard? Had EliteXC really found a doctor who would
clear Shamrock to fight? Was the main event off? Polly kept
popping up behind me to peer at the screen of my laptop, at
mixedmartialarts.com, where all threads of fact and fiction are
woven together for anonymous fandom to consider, accept,
and discredit at the speed of light. A glance at Derek and Zack
and they simply shrugged.

The CBS broadcast was to begin at 9:00 P.M., and as the
clock ticked to 6:40 the first bouts got underway. The arena
was mostly empty, but those already in their seats were there
for the fighters at the bottom of the card, the family, friends,
and teammates thrilled to say their so-and-so had fought at
the same event as the big boys. Two mismatches and one brief
battle later and still no official announcement, although the
scuttlebutt circulating was that Seth, a UFC veteran and *Ultimate Fighter* castoff, had gotten the green light, the result of
piles of money dumped at Kimbo's feet. But no one knew for
sure. Next up on the bout sheet laying out the order of fights
was Seth's original scheduled match-up, and that one was

skipped over. Erstwhile Octagon attraction Tito Ortiz appeared in the audience, wearing a garish three-piece suit and mobbed by adoring fans, and old-school pro wrestler Hulk Hogan took a seat near the cage. Within, two fighters waged a bloody war—bloody the way hitting a kitten with a golf club is bloody, bloody the way launching a rocket-propelled grenade into the refrigerator of a Red Cross blood bank is bloody. Then, a Brazilian female Muay Thai kickboxing demoness named Cyborg fed a Japanese female grappler enough fist salad to warrant both the unanimous decision and the (now full) crowd's endearing and everlasting love.

The clock struck 9:00 and the live CBS broadcast kicked off. At a live event, fans in attendance are treated to bouts that they may or may not care about before the cameras roll, and when the cameras are rolling the action is interspersed with pauses for unseen commercials and moments of deep reflection by the microphone-wielding announcers. For this Elite-XC, a remarkably polished promotion thanks to the skills of the production team and the high bar set by network television, the broadcast began with an opening montage on the big screens hanging in the arena. Then it was the official announcement that Seth, described as some kind of karate champ, was the man who would indeed step in to save the show. Shamrock, speaking backstage with a lens in his face, lamented his injury, and the crowd, numbering over 9,000, was none too pleased (this was the first they were learning of it).

In the cage, a lanky, muscular, and friendly UFC veteran named Benji beat a Brazilian into a living death, bouncing the head of the fighter called Ninja against the canvas like a basketball. In the cage, a woman named Gina Carano—EliteXC's second biggest star and the face of female mixed martial arts—clobbered a Minnesota girl until the final bell tolled. (The organization can now boast a bout between Carano and the aforementioned Brazilian demoness as their next big attraction; at Carano's introduction, the crowd's rabid screaming had reached such a fevered pitch that not a soul in the world could ever doubt the 141-pound fighter's level of stardom.) In the cage, a former UFC champ knocked out a former International Fight League champ. A 170-pound West Coast jiu-jitsu pretty boy raped a British striker, tying him in knots and defending his EliteXC welterweight crown.

Then it was the main event.

A photographer saddled up beside me, aiming his lens and dialing in adjustments like a sniper perched on a Baghdad rooftop. EliteXC event staff handed out placards that read "Kick Ass Kimbo," and the audience, on its feet, wielded them as prefabricated testaments to their passion and fervor. At any show, the moment before the main event is the most alive, the most electric, but this, this calm before the tsunami hit, was the collective inhalation before a gargantuan scream. Behind me, Polly flittered about. Derek stared out from under the brim of his cap. Zack and his camera were locked and loaded. On the big screens, a lengthy video introduction spewed bare-knuckle boxer and street fighter propaganda, preaching to a choir of zealots all ready to tumble to the floor and speak in tongues. And when Kimbo appeared with his entourage, making his way to the cage, the choir did just that. Thanks to Fort Lauderdale's close proximity to Miami and Kimbo's backyard, it was shark feeding frenzy, Death Star explosion, and borderline riot all in one, and if God truly cared about worshipping false idols, most in the arena would've been struck dead. Forget his reception at the Pru-

dential Center in Newark. Forget his reception at the Cage
Fury Fighting Championship in Atlantic City. This one won
by vicious ground and pound.

The purple-and-black-haired Seth was introduced and
anyone with even a passing knowledge of MMA knew him
as an experienced B-level fighter very capable of throwing
kicks and punches. Kimbo's entourage had spread out around
the cage, each wearing a blue "TapOut" shirt (the EliteXC
superstar's sponsorship contract with the TapOut clothing
line was rumored to hover around a million bucks), and they
heckled and shouted promises of doom like thugs. Seth
ignored them. The referee, Tony Waugh, brought the two combatants together for a brief staredown, Kimbo clearly shorter
but broader and a thousand times more menacing, and when
Waugh signaled for them to start, hundreds upon hundreds
of cameras started clicking amidst innumerable cheers.

"Watch this," said the photographer beside me, who,
based on who from within the industry had come up and
shaken his hand, knew more than most. He informed me that
Icey Mike had demanded Kimbo be paid more to face Seth,
that EliteXC had agreed to a paycheck of 700 grand, and that
Seth was going to wreck him. I turned back to watch what
was, at that instant, the exact center of the mixed martial arts
universe.

One front kick to slow down Kimbo's bull rush, one jab
on the chin to send Kimbo facefirst to the canvas, a barrage of
short punches, and the referee stepped in. In only fourteen
seconds the twenty-nine-year-old last-minute replacement
from Orlando had won.

Kimbo was dazed, so much so that he was struggling to
take down the ref. Seth howled and flexed and ran around

the cage in elation while, outside, Shaw's son, Jared, now the public face of the promotion's management and vocal opponent of all things UFC, screamed at the referee and at the very real, very fatal blow EliteXC had been dealt. Kimbo's entourage went berserk with insults and threats, and crumpled placards rained down on us as angry fans shouted their disapproval. Seth, who would later claim that his family had been threatened by members of his opponent's crew and that he had feared for his own safety, immediately shifted from celebration mode to 100 percent respect. Kimbo regained his senses, and when a microphone was thrust into his face, he let the world know that "it's all good. It's all good."

But it wasn't. As the audience filtered out on the last EliteXC event before the beast known as bankruptcy reared its ugly head, CBS executives wavered in their decision to purchase what was now a tainted product. In a day, Seth would allege on a morning radio show that he had been offered extra money to refrain from taking Kimbo down (where Kimbo's grappling is weaker), and despite a ratings count of 6.451 million viewers, ranking Kimbo versus Seth as the third most-watched U.S. mixed martial arts bout of all time, the threat of an investigation by the Florida commission as well as EliteXC's now-tarnished image made the idea of infusing the organization with cash unpalatable and unwise. The saviors fled.

Backstage at the post-fight press conference, in a room packed with various journalists and fighters, Seth stood at the podium and smiled. Kimbo sported a decent-sized shiner under one eye but the man with the purple and black hair looked untouched. "I guess I should thank Ken Shamrock," he said. And for all intents and purposes, EliteXC was dead.

V

Within days of Kimbo's fall, EliteXC had cancelled all future shows and closed up shop. I called Turi, one of the sputtering organization's executives (vice president of Getting Stuff Done), and asked him what, in his mind, had gone wrong. "I would say having upper management that wasn't as familiar with MMA as they needed to be," he said. "And definitely overspending. Trying to get too big, way too quickly."

When our paths had crossed at Soboba Casino in the desert of California back in 2001, Turi was a production assistant for the successful West Coast regional promotion King of the Cage, handing out press passes and doing whatever it took to keep the show running and running smoothly. He had later transitioned to the role of Pride executive (when that organization was the UFC's main competitor and one, true threat), and after Pride fell he was scooped up by Shaw. Now, Turi's voice betrayed a disbelief that something with as much potential as EliteXC could crash and burn. "With the amount of money we spent on things . . . it's really hard to imagine, looking back on it," he said. "But a lot of people spoke with a lot of authority on things, and obviously the decisions weren't correct. The company was very well-funded and should have been around for a long time."

What should EliteXC have done differently to avoid the iceberg? Turi knew. Knew all too well. "I think they should have focused more on the live events," he said. "To run a series of well-run, well-operated MMA events with a budget in mind and having the right staff on board, having a lean crew and everyone knowing their responsibilities . . . We could've done these shows for a long, long time. There was good staff. There really, really was good staff. Not all of it was great, but there were a lot of very knowledgeable people on the fight team. I just think had we focused on those and not tried to attack the UFC . . . We didn't need to do that. All we had to do was focus on our business and do what we needed to do and grow our brand with Showtime and CBS."

With two of the top-three most-watched bouts on his résumé, Kimbo's future couldn't possibly hold too much gloom, and when the news of EliteXC's demise broke, I called Icey Mike to get his perspective. "I don't know. I just found out about all this yesterday," he said. "All this happened yesterday and I don't know what's going on until I meet with [EliteXC] and figure out where we're at. We've got to talk to [EliteXC] and see where we're at with the contracts and stuff. We've never been in this kind of situation before."

Kimbo's return to the cage, though inevitable, looked to be a while off, as Icey Mike described a road map that no longer applied. "Our plan was to fight again in January or February, but it doesn't look like that's happening now," he said, but he didn't rule out the possibility of Kimbo fighting in the Octagon at some point if the right offer was made. "When everything is said and done, we'll take offers from anyone."

Icey Mike was, however, well-aware of how appealing his ward's pre-packaged star status was to would-be promoters, and if his shrewd moves at securing Kimbo as much money as possible for his disproportionate level of fame were of any indication, salad days would always loom. The only question was who would pay and when. "It's going to be hard for anybody to start an organization from the ground up now," he said. "These guys had a lot going for them and even they couldn't make it work."

* * *

It only took nine months for Icey Mike's ward to return to the cage, though, and this cage had eight sides. And thanks to the presence of Kimbo Slice, the most watched MMA (and underground) fighter of all time, the ratings for the tenth season of *The Ultimate Fighter* were astronomical. His official UFC pay-per-view debut took place almost a year later.

SUBMISSION ATTEMPTS

When a boxing writer or other greenhorn crosses over into no man's land and gives this new sport a try, he invariably misses the submission attempts—the subtle shifts in weight, the hand placement, the positioning, where one fighter is jockeying for a move like a choke or a lock that could end it all suddenly, and nothing compares to the exclamation point of an unconscious opponent or broken limb. But you have to know them to see them, and most don't even know what they're looking at, still stuck on the whole two-men-grabbing-and-holding-each-other homophobia and left uncomfortable in their chairs. After my glowing report on UFC 34 (Zuffa's first homerun; UFC 33 was dismal), the company asked me to show the fresh meat journos around and I did, at UFC 37 in Louisiana, practically taking a *London Times* reporter by the hand and introducing him to every fighter I saw. Still, he knew nothing. And for years, that nothingness remained the status quo, a status quo that reared its head when the "Zuffa Myth" began making the rounds, every mainstream news outlet waxing on and on how the company turned the franchise around by implementing rules, ignorant of the fact that those rules—mandatory weight classes and a long list of fouls—were the brainchild of New Jersey's Nick

Lembo and Larry Hazzard, Sr., and used by another promoter first. Anyone who perpetuated the Zuffa Myth earned
themselves the instant label of "tool," both in the sense that
they were being used and in the sense that they were idiots,
the truth just another submission attempt that reporter never
saw. But, with time, that knowledge baseline changed, the
depth of the media types involved changing like the depth
of the athletes involved, and just looking at who stepped into
the cage in that first UFC compared to who competes in it
now is like looking at a side-by-side comparison of a Nean-
derthal and an astrophysicist.

It's been said that you can always gauge the scope of an
MMA reporter's knowledge by the things he doesn't see, and
though I don't for a second believe I've seen it all, I know I've
at least seen a lot of it. Every pro show in New Jersey, every
underground show in New York City and even those unsanctioned gems that Big Dan used to organize back before the
commission in the Garden State gave a crap, dozens of UFCs,
plus other monumental events worth shelling out the dough
for a plane ticket, countless interviews and casual backstage
discussions, the words a fighter or coach will deposit in your
lap as he heads to or fro, "God, why do I do this?" or "Fuck
this cheap-ass promoter." Go to enough of them and it
becomes your scene, one great social of gossip and gabbing,
the post-show experience in New Jersey incomplete until
Lembo invites you to a nearby pub just off the boardwalk in
Atlantic City, where the referees and part-time inspectors who
are full-time cops will talk about the fighters and ring card
girls they recognize from prostitution busts. You see so much,
sometimes too much behind the curtain and behind the
scenes for it to be fun, or worth it, and when it's no longer
worth it, that's when you start losing colleagues who are

sometimes the only people who truly understand why you do it in the first place.

Anil was a law school student when I first met him, going to events with his camera for credentials and extra cash, taking shots of Octagon action when the UFC came to the Tristate, then doing smaller regional ones, settling down with the Underground Combat League and, like me, digging it. Really digging it. Becoming a full-fledged attorney did nothing to cool his passion, he still makes it to nearly every show, as much a fixture as Peter in his judo gi and Peter's lackeys at the door. If the cliché about pictures and a thousand words is true, my ink on the UCL amounts to nothing compared to his, he and I professional spectators, paid to watch and relay how freakin' cool it was to see chubby Chris become serious fighter Chris, or that scary dude covered in tattoos (even on his face, Sekou Mau-Mau was his name) get KO'd in seconds.

There are others, too, future legends of pen and paper, like Josh Gross, the sport's first real superstar journalist, and the historian Eddie Goldman, eccentric Eddie, always with a mouthful of venom for "The Man," but so jam-packed with insight it literally makes his hair stand up. Without them, I'd have never known how sharp and pointed my inquiries had to be. And of course there's Jeff Sherwood and Greg Savage, friendly and jovial and forever a part of the media establishment. When the UFC came to Miami, they were out the night before with an MMA team from California, Jeff and Greg smashing locals with chairs and kicking out teeth when some fools thought it'd be cool to brawl with real fighters. (I missed that one, I was too busy cruising down Washington Avenue in a rented convertible and, anyway, I got the excited and giggle-filled lowdown from those fighters cageside the next day.)

You'd never see Josh, Eddie, Jeff, or Greg at an underground event, though, their realm only the bright lights and big crowds of the huge shows, and I often wonder if they know what they've missed. Sometimes it's the little things that are the most interesting.

I see a ringside judge I haven't seen for a while and walk over to him, the pre-show social time when everyone says their "hellos" and catches up, and it's New Jersey, so unless there's a pay-per-view broadcast schedule that needs to be adhered to, as a rule these things always start late. The judge is Brazilian, big and burly yet welcoming and open when he smiles, which is often, and his position with the athletic commission takes up only a fraction of his time—he runs a jiu-jitsu school and is a police officer in one of the most crime-ridden cities in the country. I ask him how he's been and he shows me the months-old scars on his hands where surgery was needed to help mend broken bones. "I lost it, man. Got too emotional." He describes a domestic dispute call, a mother beaten to a bloody pulp and the assailant high on PCP and attacking him. He's a black belt in a grappling style meant for subduing anyone . . . and he broke his hands punching a bad guy on the street into oblivion. We laugh together at the irony, the joke on him and the bones in his hands, the joke on us all who think MMA imparts upon us some sort of special knowledge about fighting. It does, but it doesn't. I'm not ashamed to admit that when Craig Kukuk and Renzo first brought Brazilian Jiu-Jitsu to New York City in the mid-nineties, I was one of the clowns who took my newfound knowledge to other schools and applied it to practitioners of other styles, getting tossed about by judoka and sambo players but arm-barring and choking them whenever it went to the ground. However, that was within the confines of a gym, not an MMA bout, and in the end so much of it is mental anyway.

When Eminem's *8 Mile* track was new and cool, no less than six fighters played it for their entrance music at a Reality Fighting event in Wildwood, walking from the locker room to the ring as Eminem's words went from tentative to forceful and angry. No less than six times, and by then we were chuckling, a running gag, Anil laughing as he snapped pics of the fighters on their way to throwing down. But that walk is something few of us would ever know. I came into this sport a scrawny club kid, a fanboy with a tape recorder and questions and completely out of place, but years of close proximity to so many tough bastards and I look a lot less like a Twilo denizen. Still, despite my share of scars (staph on my leg from grappling, a nasty one on my brow), I can say I have no taste for it. An ad on Craigslist had me visiting the Fighthouse once to spar with a Wing Chun practitioner named Mustapha, and when he said "go easy" I agreed, jumped up, wrapped my legs around him, and pulled him down, the gentlest of techniques to get someone to the mat because gravity is dragging them down on top of you. But Mustapha tried to hold me up and his leg snapped, a tibia and fibula jutting angrily from his skin and reshaping the contours of his track pants, his scream and wail after I accidently broke his leg enough for me to know that I just don't have the fighting bug in me. Those wounded animal noises he made stayed with me for months.

But it's erroneous to think we journos need to have fought to be able to convey some of the magic we witness. I know how special it was to have seen Kaream defeat the monstrous Bryan or watch Joe and Kirkland go to war. It doesn't take any particular brand of insight or perception to recognize that James and Mike and Lyman and Chris were all studs. And even a blind man could recognize that, for every MMA star you see on pay-per-view or SpikeTV or CBS, there's a world of heroes out there deserving of kudos and getting none.

Backstage at Boardwalk Hall on a Friday night in February, and the atmosphere is a mixture of calm before the storm and levity. Tonight, the inaugural (and only) World Cage-fighting Alliance event has attracted over two thousand fans and packed them into chairs and bleachers around a large cage, and the main attraction sits and jokes as a teammate wraps his hands and a commission inspector looks on. In a short while, the twenty-six-year-old will warm up and then make his way from backstage to center stage. In a short while, he'll clash with a black belt from Brazil and UFC veteran. But whether he tastes victory or is force-fed defeat, the twenty-six-year-old's status as pioneer and enduring New Jersey tough guy will remain untouched, and rightfully so, for he's fought in nearly every regional New Jersey promotion since as far back as 1999, and he's even tasted combat within the Octagon himself. To know him, to look at his record and see where he's been and who he's fought, is to touch a common thread of everyone ever a part of Northeast mixed martial arts.

Some believe that grassroots MMA in the United States originated on the West Coast and migrated east, but history tells a much different tale. Consider this: the UFC debuts on pay-per-view in 1993, yet it isn't until 1997 that underground affairs like Kage Kombat and Neutral Grounds sprout up in California, and ongoing West Coast Indian Reservation fight show King of the Cage doesn't see life until 1999. On the East

Coast, however, Big Dan begins promoting unsanctioned fight cards in Northern New Jersey in 1997. Called BAMA Fight Night (BAMA stood for Bayside Academy of Martial Arts—Big Dan's school), these early events were where it all began for so many fans and fighters, and if you are fortunate enough to be there, you could see the likes of Matt and Nick Serra and a host of other future stars getting their first taste of combat in the ring. BAMA Fight Night closes up shop in 2003 thanks to the efforts of a rival promoter, but by then others have snatched up the baton and run with it.

In 2000, the first New Jersey state-sanctioned MMA bout is held on one of Lou's kickboxing cards, and soon after the New Jersey State Athletic Control Board adopts the Unified Rules (compared to Nevada and California sanctioning the sport in 2001 and 2005, respectively). The floodgates are suddenly opened. Thus far, the UFC has been to the Garden State only eight times, but through the years there have been a number of International Fight League events, Mixed Fighting Championships, and tons of regional pro shows too numerous to list. Add to that the events at Mohegan Sun casino in Connecticut (UFCs, IFLs, etc.) and the wealth of low- to mid-level MMA shows in Massachusetts, as well as the countless sanctioned amateur affairs cranking out fight cards every couple months, and you should have a clearer grasp as to the sport's scope on the Atlantic Ocean-side of the country.

"Good," says the fighter when asked how he feels. In Boardwalk Hall's ballroom, fans are being treated to a bloody slugfest between Doug and a fireplug from the Jersey Shore, but the audience's cheers and yells are muted here within the building's bowels. Instead, there's the sound of little Steve DeAngelis warming up, the staccato *whap-whap-whap* of gloves on focus mitts and measured breaths, in and out, in and out. There's the sound of grunts as Anthony the UCL alum grapples lightly with a training partner, working to get the blood flowing. "I'm good," says the twenty-six-year-old, and there's no doubt of that. He's been here many times before.

Nicknamed "The Story," the tale of the fighter's career trajectory confounds the usual "work your way up through the minor leagues" route. After an inauspicious and rocky start at BAMA Fight Night, he learns to parlay his ability to throw down into some serious fisticuffs in the ring, and by 2002 is fighting in Ring of Combat. When the UFC comes to Connecticut he is thrust into the Octagon, too soon for the twenty-one-year-old Pitts Penn representative, and though at the post-fight presser he says that it was at least a valuable learning experience, whatever it is he learned would make him a perpetual top local guy unable to pull off that crucial win when it matters. Beat the Story and you've got a slot in the UFC. But when does the gatekeeper get to come back inside? Forever a cornerstone of Northeast MMA, forever a draw, and forever considered an upper-echelon fighter, he's stuck playing the role of springboard. Can he ever break out of that?

The houselights are down in the main hall and the spotlight bathes him in white as he makes his way to the cage. A few strides behind are his teammates—the elite Brazilian Jiu-Jitsu trainer Ricardo Almeida (under whom the Story now trains), close friend and UFC star Frankie, and a who's who of skilled Garden State warriors—and all seem sure. Confident. In the cage is the Brazilian, cut from the UFC for two consecutive losses but here to work his way back, and after the Story enters and does a circuit, acknowledging his foe as he goes past, Big Dan calls things to order. Waits for the signal. Orders them to fight. The fighter has competed in nearly every major and regional promotion there's ever been on the East Coast since his first bout at BAMA Fight Night, a fixture of flesh and blood and fists and submissions, and when the Brazilian knocks him out in the second round with a hellacious right hand, Big Dan is there, leaning over the fallen combatant when he regains his senses, just as he's always done since the Story began.

The Story will be back. There's no doubt about that. As for the victorious Brazilian, he returns to the UFC in six months.

Some things just stick with you, always, like the details of a recurring nightmare or an unsettling snapshot of suffering, and for me it's Jesse from the Midwest crying out—not really crying out, more like howling in complete and utter agony. I'm ringside for an International Fight League event at the Izod Center, mid-conversation with the interim commissioner of New Jersey while within the ropes Jesse is standing above a rangy Brazilian, punching as the Brazilian snakes himself around one of Jesse's legs. The move is called a kneebar, similar to an armlock except for the obvious difference in limbs, but the idea is the same: to hyperextend the joint. It's a high-risk move, as they're easy to see coming and avoid and you can eat a lot of leather when going for it, which Jesse is making sure the Brazilian does, fist after fist after fist. Yet it truly is a chess match when grappling is introduced into a fight, and when Jesse throws one punch too many, when he should be taking the time to redistribute the weight on his legs and maybe shuck his opponent's hips off his knee joint, it's suddenly the Brazilian moving into checkmate. Do that technique to an arm and the pain kicks in well in advance, giving you enough time to tap out before it breaks; do that move to a leg and the pain doesn't kick in until it's almost too late, and when Jesse lets out an ear-piercing scream, "too late" is a sign disappearing in his rearview mirror as his car does 110 down the highway.

A hush falls over the arena, and of course we're all instantly riveted, to the pain and the crescendo of violence, to Jesse, to the Brazilian, and to the third man in the ring. Kevin Mulhall is the referee for this one, and it's as if he freezes—not out of shock or indecision, but because Jesse hasn't tapped out. Jesse hasn't even fallen yet, maybe isn't even in his right mind to remember that he can tap out, too primal and wounded animal, so it's an eternity of echoed scream and pervading horror, a moment in time suspended like a slow-motion crash on the Garden State Parkway where you know that once everything finally comes to a rest there'll be carnage and twisted and torn bodies strewn along the side of the road. And then, finally, Jesse drops to the canvas, taps out, and the Brazilian releases just as Kevin reaches down with both hands to pull them apart.

I'm not sure if the Brazilian celebrates his victory. I'm too enthralled by the swarming of officials and medical personnel around Jesse and buzzing like flies on rotten meat, and it takes me a while to process and digest the sequence of events, the scream and all the sheer pain it conveyed, stuck and taking time for my brain to swallow.

I've witnessed countless injuries. At the UCL, a fighter, skilled in grappling and a veteran of many a BAMA Fight Night, refused to tap and had his arm bent too far, and once Peter stepped into the ring with two deep-set black eyes from a broken nose sustained in training and he subsequently bled everywhere round after round, and at a sanctioned event in Boston a female competitor ate a pair of lefts that made her incoherent for hours after. Yet Jesse and his reaction to that kneebar will stick with me forever—it was immediate, raw, complete. He was upright minutes later (maybe five?), limping severely and grimacing his way out of the ring, but nothing was mitigated by that fact. Nothing at all.

In my car, parked outside of a local emergency room before UFC 32 with Pat Miletich in the passenger seat and kindly Tom Tourette's behind us spewing forth an unbridled stream of obscenities. Pat's cut too much weight and he's sick, drained, and empty, and Tom Tourette, a part-time fighter and full-time paramedic, is about to sweet-talk himself into the ER to snag a bag of saline, an intravenous boost to help Pat replace those precious lost fluids. The legendary UFC fighter takes the tiny disco ball dangling from the rearview mirror in his hand, says "Nice disco ball," with a grin. In a few hours Pat will be facing Shonie Carter in the Octagon, and he's in no condition to fight now, the desperation of his predicament forcing me—the only journo sitting nearby in the hotel lobby with a car parked outside—to act as taxi driver. Not that I mind helping out. But considering the company, the dangling disco ball is suddenly . . . embarrassing. And all I can manage is a meek "Uh, thanks."

Why cover mixed martial arts and not something more socially acceptable, like baseball or football? Or at least more legal, like boxing or vanilla martial arts? For me, the answer is the thrill, of course. Watch it on TV and maybe you get it. The referee's signal and the fighters, larger than life, perhaps one of them is an Olympic gold medalist in Greco-Roman wrestling, perhaps the other is a world champion in kick-boxing or jiu-jitsu. At the referee's signal, the fighters engage and your stomach gets tight and full of butterflies. Watching it from cageside (or ringside, depending on the promotion), though, within range of the flying sweat and droplets of blood, the sounds of the leather gloves hitting flesh and the grunts, well, that's another thing entirely. At an event at the Taj Mahal in Atlantic City, a grappling specialist from Washington wraps his arms around a Russian and the two fall against the ropes, and I can tell who hasn't showered that day. At an event at a recreation center in Elizabeth, New Jersey, a scrapper from Tiger Schulmann's Karate trades blows with a lanky kickboxer and future *The Ultimate Fighter* contestant, and my notebook is suddenly splattered with crimson. At the MGM Grand Garden Arena in Vegas, I'm close enough to see Hawaiian phenom B.J. Penn knock out Japanese fighter Caol Uno with such force that Uno's eyes point in two different directions, the star from the Land of the Rising Sun now motionless against the chain-link fence. This goes beyond the mere tightening of the stomach and the butterflies. This is fight-or-flight, gladiator combat, pure kinetic art form painted with broad strokes all rolled into one. If junkies could somehow put it into a needle, they'd shoot and score, shoot and score, and hunt for more.

There is, unfortunately, a downside to getting that close. That close and you can see behind the curtain. That close and these guys aren't fighters but real people, people with hopes and dreams, and simple statistics dictate that half of them are going home that night with those hopes and dreams taking a major hit. Sure, it's one thing if someone trained wrong or didn't train hard enough. That's their fault. It's another thing if they trained smart and trained hard and despite it all still got their asses kicked. A "you got beaten by a better man" loss and a "sorry, man, you were just unlucky" loss are both still losses no matter which way you try to spin it. When you wake up to being carried out of the cage strapped to a back-board, when you're stuck sitting in the waiting area of an emergency room holding an ice pack to your hyper-extended elbow, or the MRI reveals your ACL and MCL now resemble so much ripped upholstery, your ass is no less kicked.

It's rough seeing that because, try as hard as you might, you can't stop yourself from caring about these people. When Matt Hughes knocked out Carlos Newton by dropping him on his head, thereby winning the UFC welterweight champi-onship belt, I jumped up with elation and screamed at the top of my lungs (not my finest hour in terms of professionalism). Sitting in the press row doesn't make you immune to emo-tion or somehow kill your empathy. Hughes was just a farm-boy then, and when we sat chatting in a hotel lobby the night before, he admitted he was ready to give up on mixed martial arts if his big break didn't come soon, and it's impossible to not let those details get to you. And that eccentric fighter on the tail end of his career, that fighter with the sick daughter, that fighter with the aspirations of somehow making a living off this "MMA thing," it's painful seeing them fail and it's hard not to get caught up in it. At UFC 38, at the Royal Albert Hall in London, England, British heavyweight Ian Freeman pounded out jiu-jitsu monster Frank Mir in a bout Mir was supposed to win and win easily. But Freeman had done it, and when he was handed the microphone, he dedicated the bout to his sick father—who, unbeknownst to him but known to us in the press section, had already passed on. My Brit cohort Jim Burman looked at me then with tears in his eyes.

Sometimes it's impossible not to care.

11

"Ground and pound." The technique, the mode of combat where you take your opponent down to the ground (really, the canvas) and pound on him from above. In the UFC, champs are crowned who specialize in this, and Lyman utilizes a hellacious ground and pound to batter Doug en route to a unanimous decision victory at the Cage Fury Fighting Championships. Ground and pound is what Emerson does to Angel at that UCL in the Bronx. Ground and pound is what Tom does to Igor Gracie, because, really, he'd be hard-pressed to pull off a submission on such an accomplished Brazilian Jiu-Jitsu master and it's much easier to just repeatedly punch someone in the face, feeding them leather until they tap the mat with their hand, or the referee pries you off saying, "Okay, that's enough, you win," or the clock runs out and the judges tallying up the score cards award you the decision. You lose by ground and pound and you're coming away with a nice array of abrasions and bruises and cuts, and maybe your girlfriend or mother won't cry when she sees you afterward, but there's a good chance she won't be able to hold it in. You lose by ground and pound, and—while not quite the exclamation point of a knockout that sends you into instant dreamland, or a submission move you never see coming and has you screaming in pain before you can even tap—everyone knows your opponent has put his stamp on you. Like some bipedal Texas longhorn steer that fancies himself a fighter, you've been branded.

The natural progression for anyone too good at wrestling in high school or college and unwilling to forsake that talent for a job in the real world, a job that doesn't involve takedowns and reversals, is to give mixed martial arts a try. Never mind the Olympics. Never mind professional wrestling. Too few slots there make it a statistical improbability, and the idea of getting paid maybe a couple hundred bucks (and then a thousand to a million after a few years and some luck) to add punches and weird submission moves to those single-leg and double-leg takedowns, those gut wrenches and cradles, makes for one heck of an appealing option. Like the journey from *Homo erectus* to *Homo sapien*, only with more cheering and bloody noses. In fact, go to any MMA show at any level and take a poll as to who hails from a wrestling background; the numbers will boggle your mind. A wrestler is born, learns to crawl, learns to walk, learns to shoot for takedowns and sprawl, then transitions to mixed martial arts.

Frankie is no different. In July 2005, Frankie parlays a wrestling background from Toms River High School East and Clarion University of Pennsylvania into a dominant performance at a UCL in the Bronx, battering a national-level Greco-Roman wrestler with enough brutality and finality that referee Jerry steps in and ends it. It's Frankie's first venture in the realm of mixed martial arts, and though it will be his only time competing at Peter's underground event, it's number one in a long line of ground-and-pound beatdowns the 155-pound powerhouse delivers on the road to the Ultimate Fighting Championship. Family, friends, and fans will turn out in droves to see him compete in New Jersey's minor league promotions—a Ring of Combat at Asbury Park, a Sportfighting in Hoboken, a Reality Fighting in Atlantic City—and by February 2007, Frankie, one of the Garden State's biggest ticket sellers, a wrestler who got the memo and learned to box and avoid jiu-jitsu black belt-level submissions, is in Las Vegas, stepping into the hallowed and sacred turf called the Octagon.

I'm ringside for a show called "World's Best Fighter," a one-shot MMA event at Boardwalk Hall in Atlantic City pitting a team of competitors from South Korea against a team of Americans (mostly locals). Team Asia is getting its ass kicked, and the Korean contingent of fans has sat mostly silent in the section behind me, stoic in the face of defeat, or disinterested, or both. Frankie is thousands of miles away at this very moment at the Mandalay Bay Events Center, taking on an undefeated West Coast fighter while here on the East Coast Frankie's teammate, K-Rod, is about to step through the ropes to face off against another overmatched Korean. Tom, cornering K-Rod and two steps behind, looks at his phone and grins. "I just got the text," Tom turns to me and says. "Frankie won by unanimous decision. Beat the crap out of him for all three rounds!" I scream out a "Yes!" and pump my fist into the air, and moments later the ring announcer is handed a slip of paper. He reads it, pausing in his fighter introductions to say, "New Jersey's own Frankie Edgar has just won his UFC debut." Cheers erupt from the audience.

Three years later Frankie is the champ.

BAMA FIGHT NIGHT

"**I** believe that the moment New York State starts to regulate the sport, the underground will become history," said Melvina at a legislative roundtable in downtown Manhattan. Around us in the conference room: Jeff Blatnik, anti-MMA proponent Assemblyman Bob Reilly, pro-MMA proponent Assemblyman Steve Englebright, UFC exec Marc Ratner, and a host of curious, myself included. It was the New York State Athletic Commission Chairwomen's turn with the imaginary conch shell, so Melvina was offering up her two cents.

"These people are fighting underground because they can't fight anywhere else," she said. "I believe that if they have an opportunity to do it on a legal basis, above board, they will then prefer to do it in a much more regulated manner."

And she was right. It didn't take a crystal ball to see what was to come. Really, all you needed to do was to look across the Hudson, to New Jersey and what happened when the sport was legalized there. All you needed to know was contained in the tale of BAMA Fight Night.

My first BAMA Fight Night was in 2002, and already there'd been a score of them, beginning in 1997 and recurring like some ancient, vengeful god's fevered dreams of violence and battle. It wasn't quite illegal when it began, merely unsanctioned, existing in a nebulous realm (its competitors were unpaid) and nestled between "needed" and "tolerated." Before Lou's tentative forays into MMA, it was the only game in town in New Jersey when so many were eager and desperate to play. Driving to that middle school in Plainfield, I at least had an idea of what to expect; Big Dan advertised his events on his website, and by then I'd been to a number of UFCs and one grassroots show, a no-nonsense affair in a high school gymnasium in Richmond, Virginia. There would be fights of varying degrees of skill and intensity, there would be intimacy—if you had to you could leave your seat in the bleachers and reach out and tap a fighter on the shoulder as he sat on his stool in his corner—and there would be scared mothers and proud fathers and assorted family members with more than just a vested interest in the outcome of each bout. The maestro of it all was Big Dan.

Snapshot of Big Dan, a.k.a. "Big" Dan Miragliotta: musclebound, bald-headed with a warm, broad smile and keen, thoughtful eyes. In 2002 he was thirty-nine years old, but come 2010 he is refereeing in the UFC, traveling the globe to wherever the Octagon is erected, and that, coupled with a lengthy career officiating bouts in New Jersey and up and down the Eastern Seaboard, has made him the third man in the cage for anywhere from eight hundred to a thousand fights. Big Dan's got over thirty years of martial arts training, competing, and teaching under his belt—when Renzo fought in Japan for the first time, the Garden State native was brought along as his Muay Thai coach—but to anyone even remotely familiar with the sport on the East Coast, the "man with the tan" (Lembo's words, not mine) made his first, most poignant mark on MMA with BAMA Fight Night.

I parked, and in the lot around me were cars bearing the stickers and decals of martial arts schools on their windows, places I'd heard of (Renzo Gracie Academy, Combined Martial Arts, Bayside Academy of Martial Arts, Team Endgame, Pitts Penn, Fight Factory) and places that were new to me (Tong Dragon, Fatjo Martial Arts Center, Extreme Martial Arts, Planet Jiu-Jitsu, Alex Wilkie). It was like reading the recipe for a soup, full of ingredients I only partially recognized, the end product filling and tasting of combat.

Inside the South Plainfield Middle School a blond mom greeted me, checked my name off a list, and told me I could wander, so I did. In the cafeteria, Big Dan made a list of names of all the fighters who had shown up (a list sometimes far different from those who had promised to come), and as the fighters and their coaches and teammates milled about anxiously, match-ups were made.

Eddy was there with his guys, who included the diminutive Glenn, an ace with leglocks who looked like "Superman" in his red shorts and blue shirt and kneepads.

Karem was there, too, with Katz, in the zone and pacing, five months away from falling to Jose and still very motivated and hopeful. Karem's paychecks for winning those pro bouts in Atlantic City were long since spent, and to get him another paying gig Katz needed fight footage to circulate (footage the equivalent of a résumé to someone who beats on people for a living).

Big Dan came over and gave them some kid named Justin as an opponent, and made them the main event.

The rest of the bouts solidified, but there were an odd

BAMA Fight Night veteran Glenn (*left*) at the UCL. (*Jim Genia*)

number of willing and able. Big Dan needed one more fighter to make an even fourteen bouts. He turned to Mark, the leader of Pitts Penn.

Pitts Penn, hard-asses supreme. Not the most technical, sometimes they'd lose to a slick Renzo guy or some Muay Thai ace, but they were rough, hardened, the kind of men who'd have your back in a bar fight, and if you lost, the kind of men who'd run your assailant down with a truck the second he stepped out into the parking lot. New Jersey circa 2001 had its jiu-jitsu clans, its TSKers, its starry-eyed traditionalists and wannabes, but there was only one true black sheep fight team. Hells Angels with handwraps. Corsairs, brigands, highwaymen with mouthpieces. Pitts fucking Penn.

Mark looked every bit the blue collar man with a mean streak, and though he hadn't come to fight, he wasn't about to turn one down. He pulled the hood of his sweatshirt down

BAMA Fight Night veteran Glenn (*back to camera*) getting choked
at the UCL. (*Jim Genia*)

over his eyes, casting his face in shadow, and like Kaream, he,
too, began pacing. Lead by example, taken to the vicious
extreme.

Soon I was sitting in the bleachers, and after Big Dan bel-
lowed into a microphone, thanking everyone for coming and
chastising those who promised to compete but backed out,
Kevin Mulhall took over, refereeing each bout as pair after
pair of fighters stepped into the ring and fought.

Glenn needed four minutes to make his opponent submit.
Mark needed two. And after a few hours of fists flying and
bodies clashing with bodies, it was finally Kaream's turn. He
needed only two minutes as well, and when he kicked Justin
in the leg the sound of shin bone on thigh was so loud it res-
onated throughout the gymnasium.

Kaream got his footage.

Justin was one of the last people to leave the venue that
night. His parents had to carry him out.

*   *   *

So many gems then, rough and unpolished, but you could still see them glitter, still discern their worth. I heard tales of Pitts Penn legend Billy Craparo, who fought a cop in the ring and wrecked him (the words *folk hero* come to mind), and though Jose had moved on to the pros by that time, I got to see the Story slug it out with Joey the karate man, got to see Carmine slap on smooth submissions, got to see a fighting whirlwind named Jay Isip, and got to see 260-pound Carlos Moreno wreak utter devastation. Once, a big, white Irishman named Declan thought he could go toe-to-toe with Carlos, and a bald guy from Pennsylvania named Eric had similar ideas. Carlos put them both away fast, with deftness and ease and the efficiency of someone with more talent than a human being should possess. (Years later, Carlos would win the Ring of Combat heavyweight title, fracturing his opponent's orbital bone with a jab. Years after that he would be in jail, doing time for a bar fight that went too far. Tom, a training partner then, wrote "Free Carlos" on his back when he stepped into the cage for a bout.)

They would come from New York, like Chris Scanlon the union worker, or from Philadelphia, like Judah the bouncer, two men who were so nice it was hard to imagine that they could bring themselves to harm someone else. There was Gene Fabrikant, who'd managed to pull off three unsanctioned fight shows in Brooklyn before the athletic commission shut them down; Gene would bring fighters down from Brighton Beach, Russians who knew no English and spoke only sambo. I even ran into Peter there, shook his hand for the first time as he thanked me for my coverage of his first show (it was then that I was told that I would always be welcome at UCL shows).

So many gems, and yet none of us knew that there were only a few BAMA Fight Nights left.

11

"A very good friend of mine in Virginia named Gary Miles was running a show in Virginia right after the UFC had gotten banned in most states," says Big Dan. The question: how BAMA Fight Night got its start. "His was like an underground event, and I went down there and refereed for a couple of his shows. He talked me into running shows in New Jersey, so that's how I got started in Jersey. It was a place for our guys to fight. They were all training very hard. There were a lot of schools in the area, on the East Coast training. Back then it was called 'NHB' (for "no holds barred") or *vale tudo*. I decided to run a show in my school to see how it would work out, and the first event we had I only had 350 chairs for the event. We sold all 350, and we had I think eighteen or twenty fights that night. Matt Serra fought, Nicky Serra fought, a few guys from Virginia fought. And that was the beginning of BAMA Fight Night.

"We outgrew my school and after I think the third event, we started running shows at South Plainfield Middle School and South Plainfield High School," he says. "I've had Renzo Gracie, Bas Rutten, Gokor [Chivichyan], and Bart Vale all at the school at various times doing refereeing. Bas Rutten was actually the DJ at one of my events."

It was, of course, a matchmaking nightmare—the sort of thing not meant for the obsessive-compulsive or faint of heart. "It was all amateur and no one was getting paid to fight, so if you aren't getting paid, it was easy at the last minute, if you decided not to fight or if you had to work overtime or whatever the reason was, to just back out. There were no contracts. It wasn't sanctioned by anybody, so you wouldn't get penalized or blackballed if you wanted to fight again. The hardest thing was keeping the fights that were set up to be that way. Like, if 'A' was fighting 'B' and 'C' was fighting 'D,' a lot of the times 'A' would fight 'D' and 'C' was missing and I would have to call into the audience for another fighter and we would get two or three more fights." Big Dan lets out a chuckle. "We would always keep extra mouthpieces and cups because people would show up, go throw on a pair of shorts and a shirt, and next thing you know they're in the ring fighting."

Talking to him now, years after the BAMA Fight Night show and well into his career as professional referee, you get the sense that Big Dan has few regrets. There's a fondness there, a nostalgia for good times past.

I ask him which installment was his favorite. There is no hesitation.

"We had a young kid who has since passed away unfortunately—Billy Craparo," he says. "He was a tough kid, and he was challenged by one of Renzo's students named Steve Dalinger. Steve Dalinger was a cop in Middletown and Billy Craparo was the brother of a kid who was always getting in trouble in Middletown. They were kind of . . . not picking on him, just making sure he was being pushed in the right direction, but he felt he was being picked on a lot. So Dalinger challenged Billy and Billy took the fight, and he was like eighteen years old and Dalinger was about twenty-eight years old. It was the biggest event I ever had. I think we had 1,500 or a thousand spectators, half the audience was cops and corrections officers, the other half were kids and derelicts. It was a very exciting night and a lot of fun. Billy actually won that

fight and put Dalinger in the hospital for a couple days." He
pauses, then continues. "The funniest part of that show that I
remember is that I had all my students around the ring as
security because we knew there was going to be trouble
between the kids and the cops and we wanted to make sure
nothing was going to happen. After the fight was over, some
kid comes flying through my guys, slides underneath the
ropes into the ring. I turn around and I see him, and I catch
him by his shirt and his groin and I throw him over the top
rope and out of the ring. And it ended up being Billy Craparo's brother!" Big Dan laughs heartily at that. "That was
the funniest part of that show, I think."

Does he miss the BAMA Fight Night events? "Hell, yeah,
I miss them a lot. A lot of camaraderie, a lot of guys just
coming up—watching them coming up and getting better
every time they fight. It was a lot of fun. Whether you made
money or lost money at the event, just the excitement and the
fun with the new fighters was worth it."

That prompts me to ask if the events were money-makers.
"Some of them were. Like I said, we had some events with a
thousand spectators, and that's what kept my school open. At
the time I had stopped teaching kids, I was only teaching
fighters, and as most people know, to have gyms with fighters, you don't make a dime. They don't pay, half of them
don't work, so it's tough to keep a school open like that. My
events were what was keeping my doors open, and they did
for about six years."

The last BAMA Fight Night was on April 12th, 2003, and
the next scheduled event died on the vine. I ask Big Dan how
it all came to an end. The scuttlebutt at the time was that a
rival promoter was jealous at BAMA Fight Night's success,

and that said promoter made it his mission to ensure the State of New Jersey was not turning a blind eye to unsanctioned events.

"It all ended when the UFC became sanctioned in New Jersey, and the commission came down to me and said I could no longer run my shows the way I was running them and that I had to use the commission to run my shows. When you're only making 1,500 to two thousand dollars an event, and it's going to cost you another four or five to run the event, it's a no-brainer. You just don't do it. If I was going to lose money, I just decided to stop doing the shows."

(Nick Lembo further clarifies: "The shows ended after complaint letters were being written to the State Police and the Attorney General and we were forced to take immediate action. Up to that point, we were just monitoring the events and deciding how to classify and regulate them. They were not exactly pro contests in this very new sport. They had more of an amateur feel to them, as an overall event.")

Years of fights, of thrillers and raucous crowds and weekend superstars, and just like that it was over. BAMA Fight Night was history. But whatever vacuum created was filled just as quickly with sanctioned events, like the fledgling Ring of Combat and Reality Fighting, not quite the epic affairs of the UFC but enough. A few short years later came the amateur leagues. There were no underground shows—there was no need for them.

And what of Big Dan and his transition from unsanctioned promoter to card-carrying NJSACB official? "What happened then was the commission asked me if I would like to referee for them, and that's when I started refereeing for them," he says. "I think they respected me because of what

we did. Here we were, we were running an event—a successful event—it was the only one on the East Coast except
for that one in Virginia, and it was doing pretty well and we
had a lot of fighters in our stable that were coming up."

I ask how he came to be a UFC referee—considered the
pinnacle of officialdom. "They came to New Jersey about
three years ago," he says. "When they came here, our bosses,
Nick Lembo and Larry Hazzard, were adamant about using
just our officials in New Jersey. The UFC wanted to use [John]
McCarthy, Herb Dean, or Mario [Yamasaki] or anybody else,
just their guys. So when they came here we did that show,
Kevin and I, we did every fight, and they called me up for
their next event and asked if I wanted to work with them and
I said yes. I've been working with them since."

One last question, but from the animation and life in his
voice, I feel I already know the answer. I ask Big Dan if he
would do it all again, if he would wear the promoter's hat
and resurrect BAMA Fight Night, a by-the-book permutation
for this well-sanctioned era.

"Without a doubt," he says. "Without a doubt I would."

EPILOGUE

The text comes on Friday night, a short and succinct "UCL this Sunday" as I'm sitting on my couch, and minutes later comes the follow-up with location details. Seven years of writing about New York City's lone illicit fight circuit and those texts are really all I needed to know about what's in store. There will be fistfights and beatings, cringe-worthy slams and chokes, then gratitude, and when it's over there'll be the feeling that all present are in on a big, juicy secret. No clue who is fighting, though, the "who" at this point mattering much less than the where. Twentysomething shows thus far in all manner of gyms, but this one in the Bronx will be the first time that the venue is in an Islamic cultural center and mosque, worn posters advertising boxing match-ups and karate tournaments of yore traded in for walls adorned with Quranic verse and *New York Post* and *Daily News* clippings describing violence against Muslims. But that's how it goes.

Kaream called me from Rikers days before. His sentence had finally been handed down and he was going to do a year upstate on the gun charge, a welcome change of scenery and a chance for him to keep his head down and reboot, maybe introduce Kaream version 2.0 to the world upon his exit, and would his criminal record affect his ability to fight in New York when everything was legalized? I didn't know for sure, but Lembo seemed to think it wouldn't and I passed that on. The funny thing about the tap out, though, was that you always did it so you could come back and fight another day.

Anil meets me on the subway in Manhattan and we ride north, staring out the windows when the train goes above-ground, staring out at the city as dusk falls, and when our stop comes we walk the rest of the distance in the shadow of the elevated tracks. And there is Kevin at the door, with a warm and firm handshake, he doesn't even have to consult his list (really, just a piece of paper with names scribbled on it), he lets us right in.

There will be no admission charged for this one, but only a select few have been invited. Once, at an event in Queens, a limousine pulled up and out came men in tuxedos and their dates in dresses—"Just an evening at the underground show, honey. Is that cool?" This would clearly be the furthest thing from that.

Within is Chris, gone now from the New Generation Karate school and on the verge of moving to Florida, not here to fight but to watch. We clasp our right hands together and embrace with our lefts, the universal greeting for tough guys and thugs, then Peter and I shake hands. Unlike Chris, he is scheduled to compete, to mix it up with a muscle-bound bruiser named Braddock from Ozone Park for the first-ever UCL championship belt (sponsored by a clothing company called "Sadistic Athletics"). The goateed Latino is clad in a blue judo uniform, his black belt is tied around his waist. Nowadays, Peter's been teaching at a gym in Queens, laying down mats for grappling and working to get an MMA program off the ground. Training for a fight has been the furthest thing from his mind, but someone has to get into the ring and face Braddock for the belt, so why not, right? Although in this instance, "ring" is a bit of misnomer. Combatants will be doing their thing on a mat, the melee held in place by the scant observers and the natural reluctance of anyone to let the fight spill out onto the hard concrete beyond.

A speaker upstairs starts broadcasting the evening prayers and they echo throughout the building. There's the faint smell of burnt incense, of dust and mold, and the tang of the industrial-strength cleaner a young kid is using to wash the mat. Outside, a train rumbles by. Around us the cast of characters assembles.

There's Rage, the coach from Brooklyn, and his ward Rashad standing close by, Rashad still very fit and very ready. Jerome, a veteran of the last show, sits across the room, carved out of dark marble, his lips bulging with a mouthpiece as he gets acclimated to the feel of it there. There's Braddock, cool and focused and flanked by Richie Torres, Kenneth the amateur fighter, and Daniel the pro, his trainer partners at Katz's school. Add a kickboxer named John and an aggressive scrapper named Anton to the card, and there's three bouts total, an abbreviated menu but enough. All told, there's just over thirty people present, somehow each of us—the coaches and teammates, the writer and the photographer, the Sadistic Athletic reps, the brother and girlfriend of one of the fighters, the distinguished alum—at least tangentially connected to what's about to transpire. The evening prayers drone on.

In a few weeks, I will be sitting in an arena in Philadelphia for a Bellator event, watching Lyman lose for the very first time, his foe an Olympic wrestler with unstoppable takedowns.

After five rounds, both men's faces will resemble abused slabs of meat, and K-Rod and Tom, there as spectators, will come sit beside me. Their fight school has merged recently with the folks at Tiger Schulmann's, so I get to hear the ardent Jersey Shore scrappers dish insight. "The way they were in shape, I always thought they were on steroids or something," says K-Rod with a laugh. "But they're not, they just work so hard and train so much. It's freakin' nuts."

Nothing denotes acceptance like the approving nod of an experienced fighter, and K-Rod and Tom give it to the karate stylists who adapted to MMA, karate the harder, more difficult route toward viability and the exact opposite of all those wrestlers and jiu-jitsu folk learning to strike for the sake of the sport, traveling the other direction toward the same goal of well-roundedness, and how can you express anything other than admiration for what they had accomplished and how far they had come? The two marvel at the machine churning out fighters and at their new TSK brethren, at Nick (who will be fighting in the UFC in a couple months), at Jimmie (who just won a prestigious King of the Cage belt), at Louis (who was now a Ring of Combat champ). We all agree that Lyman will be back.

But that's weeks away and I'm still at the mosque. In a dark room beyond and in the shadows upstairs the fighters are warming up, hitting pads and flitting about, and then they make their way to the mat without fanfare, the referee (one of the Sadistic Athletic guys) addressing each of them and then telling us—in case we don't know—that this one is Peter and this one is Braddock. Peter, standing in one corner of the battlefield in his traditional *gi*, is one-hundred eighty-five pounds; Braddock, shirtless and in green camouflage shorts, is upwards of two-hundred twenty-five.

In theory, the shiny chunk of gold-painted hardware with "UCL CHAMPION" on it should transform this pairing between the promoter and his foe into something more than just a run-of-the-mill brawl. But so much for theory, as the bout plays out like so many have before. Although a veteran of at least three times as many underground fights, Peter's experience cannot overcome the size disadvantage, and the fact that Braddock is a compact behemoth with muscles upon muscles and is prepared to fight only makes things worse. With a wicked grin Braddock comes forward looking to throw leather, and when Peter ducks low and reaches in for a take-down, the bigger man simply pushes his hips away and lets all of his weight come down on the judo black belt's shoulders. He follows it up with a salvo of knees to the head and body while Peter is on all fours. Round 1 ends, and in the fighters' respective corners comes a stream of impassioned instructions and encouragement amidst huffing and puffing. Then Peter and Braddock are back at it, and soon Braddock is straddling Peter, raining down punches. The referee steps in when Peter taps out.

There's no doctor or nurse present, nor EMT, and the cacophony of hooting and shouts goes silent as Peter remains motionless on his back. He's taken one heck of a beating and it shows in his labored breathing and the abrasions mottling his face. Braddock, ecstatic a moment ago, is suddenly quiet, and he kneels beside his fallen opponent to offer a hand. A minute of this stretches into two. By minute four Peter's eyes are open, and he's moved to a chair and surrounded by nearly everyone and assaulted by a barrage of pats on the back and shoulders. Someone says "Good fight, Pete," and all—including Braddock—applaud.

The first-ever UCL champ is crowned.

One month before, Joe Funaro won his Asylum Fight League debut in Atlantic City with a triangle choke in just over a minute, while James found that he liked competing in an amateur promotion in Virginia. He'd racked up wins and won a tournament and was anticipating going pro down there, undaunted by the distance and the trek. There could be no questioning the brothers' abilities.

The Bronx, and Rashad and Jerome square off next, the two battling back and forth furiously. At one point Rashad has his arm snaked around his foe's neck, struggling to complete a choke, but Jerome escapes, and after the second round Rashad is too spent to come out for more. Anton is victorious as well, slamming his way out of John's choke and forcing him to submit midway through Round Two. And that's it. The show is over.

Before everyone shuffles out there are the handshakes and good-byes. Congrats are levied on the victors, and just as vigorously, "better luck next times" on the losers. John makes a point of apologizing to one and all for giving up. Jerome, meanwhile, declares that "it is officially time to get drunk."

Peter follows us out. A baseball cap sits low on his head, casting deep shadows over his battered face. If not for the disappointment in his voice, you'd never know he was on the wrong end of a beatdown. "I'll get him next time," he says, and that sentence there speaks volumes.

No one can pin down an expected date for the legalization of MMA in New York State, the matter too confusing, too embarrassing, and maybe even too painful for anyone to address without indifference rising up as a psychological defense. But legalization is inevitable. What then for the Underground Combat League?

"The UCL brand is not going anywhere," Peter once told me of the thing he had made from scratch, the enduring open secret that had served up fighting in a wasteland where few could or did. "Right now I'm just figuring out which direction the UCL will go in." He talked of finding sponsors then, of financial backers willing to take the organization into the territory of the above-the-board, fully sanctioned, and pro. But what if he couldn't find someone to help facilitate that leap? Would Peter and his baby continue on as one of the last vestiges of *vale tudo* combat in MMA world?

"We're not going to break any laws," Peter said to me, and we both laughed at that then.

"I'll get him next time," Peter says in the Bronx.

And I'm laughing still.